W9-BQI-500

The Workcamp Experience:
Involving Youth in Outreach to the Needy

By
John C. Shaw

LIBRARY
BRYAN COLLEGE
DAYTON TN 37321

Group Books

Loveland, Colorado

115545

Dedication

I dedicate this book to my wife, Nancy; our son, Randy; and our daughter, Susan. Their patience and understanding during my many years of traveling and absence from home during workcamp trips are very deeply appreciated.

The Workcamp Experience: Involving Youth in Outreach to the Needy

Copyright © 1987 by John C. Shaw

First Printing

All rights reserved. No part of this book may be reproduced in any manner whatsoever without written permission from the publisher except where noted in the text and in the case of brief quotations embodied in critical articles and reviews. For information write Permissions, Group Books, Box 481, Loveland, CO 80539.

Credits

Designed by Judy Atwood

Edited by Cindy S. Hansen

Scripture quotations are from the Holy Bible, New International Version. Copyright © 1973, 1978, 1984 International Bible Society. Used by permission of Zondervan Bible Publishers.

Library of Congress Cataloging-in-Publication Data

Shaw, John C., 1939—
    The workcamp experience.

    Bibliography: p.
    1. Work camps. 2. Youth—Religious life. I. Title.
BV4531.2.S5 1987   259'.8   87-11939
ISBN 0-931529-57-3 (soft)

Acknowledgments

Many people have contributed to the workcamp operations represented in this book. The creation and development of the program were accomplished in partnership with Thom Schultz, whose critique and insights always proved invaluable. Jeff Myers spent years of persistent hard work to develop registration and crew-assigning procedures. Lee Sparks contributed faithful effort and organizing abilities to toolroom operations and public relations. Joel Fay and Joani Schultz contributed refinements to the program as directors who constantly pursued top-quality experiences for young people.

The sense of Christian mission embedded in youth groups throughout the country has made this book possible and necessary. For those groups and leaders who dare to serve through work, this book is not only a guide, but a symbol of their dedication and commitment as Christian servants.

Special acknowledgment goes to Fred Krautwurst for his contribution of personal expertise, experience and stories of workcamping to the content of this book.

Contents

Charts

Part One

What Are Workcamps and Why Do Them?

Chapter One
What Is the Workcamp Experience?

What is the workcamp experience?
This seems a simple enough question in search of a simple answer. Not so. The workcamp experience in youth ministry is too rich, too complex and too varied from group to group (and from youth to youth) to lend itself to simple description.

Yet the question is often asked and deserves a thoughtful response. To get us started, the workcamp experience is an organized mission project in which young people and their adult leaders combine their skills and enthusiasm to repair, refurbish and renew homes of needy people. Workcamps usually span a week or two in the summer. Youth groups often travel to other states than their own to participate in either a workcamp organized by themselves or by others (e.g., denominations, Group, etc.).

This working definition may seem too simple (even perhaps boring) to the thousands of young people who have made a difference for Christ and whose lives have been changed by the workcamp experience. For example, Susan tells how the workcamp experience helped her to gain confidence:

My greatest fear was being alone in a

crowd. I had always been shy around strangers, and my greatest fear revealed my low self-esteem. Then came the summer of our work-camp. It was a special summer—a summer I will never forget. My greatest fear evaporated while I was surrounded by strangers at a work-camp in Petersburg, West Virginia.

The first night, I talked with a youth pastor I didn't even know. I was amazed at the ease with which I talked with this stranger. This was the "new me" coming out—a stronger, self-assured individual.

During the week, I worked with five other participants from different churches. Our assignment was to build a cinder-block wall behind the house of Sonny and Carol. My group was apprehensive about meeting these strangers, but the excitement of helping quickly grew on us. Soon Sonny and Carol were calling us their "kids." They were special, and they made us feel special.

At the workcamp I found strength inside me I never thought I possessed. I learned to do things independently. I found the confidence I had always lacked. Now I am prepared to meet the challenges of going to college and facing new experiences with new people. The workcamp convinced me I can handle my greatest fear and live with confidence.

I write this book with the sincere hope that it will help young people, youth groups and adult sponsors grow in faith, love and service through a workcamp experience. Whether it is a locally arranged work experience or a nationally organized workcamp, participants will be challenged to grow in faith, develop new skills, face major responsibilities and accomplish big jobs.

You can use this book as a study guide to determine if

you have the resources to organize a workcamp within your group. Or, you may decide to go to a workcamp that is already planned and arranged by others. Either way, you will be able to consider thoroughly some form of work-camping for your group. Then you can take the next steps of preparation with a clear plan in mind.

Workcamps should be a part of every youth ministry. Workcamps bring out personal strengths and Christian values in young people. During the past 15 years, I've seen shy, insecure, self-doubting, 90-pound sophomores complete a week of workcamping bursting with self-confidence. They were excited to find more ways to help other people.

I've seen burly athletes discover and express their carefully subdued sensitivity after working daily in the home of a transparently loving old man whose arms and legs were paralyzed, but whose soul was fully functioning.

I've seen 370 young people celebrate a week of stren-uous labor in heat and humidity. Their celebration ex-pressed Christian love and servanthood, commitment and understanding, awareness of their real ability to help others and a personal realization that God works wonders with willing hands.

I've seen varieties of church backgrounds, cultures, races, skill levels and expectations melt into a shared mis-sion. God's encompassing love and the presence of Jesus Christ became the focus of the individuals who united in a ministry based on the basic principles of Christian faith: love for God, neighbor and self.

Workcamps offer young people powerful experiences of Christian outreach. Kids can grow through learning first-hand how to face challenges, develop new abilities, make decisions and carry personal responsibility. Each person is responsible for a part of the total project. Each person shares the eventual satisfaction and success of the project. Each person faces the inner search for strength, skill, stamina, resourcefulness and creativity. Each person must react to the daily fluctuations and surprises of new people, new tasks and new territory.

Most of all, workcamps splash a clear picture of Jesus
and the Christian faith into the minds of young people.
Teenagers want to experience personally what they have
read about in the Bible and talked about in church. They
want to paint images of Jesus in their minds as accurately
as possible. Will their experiences today reflect the New
Testament experiences of Jesus' disciples? Or will the
young people be confused by the inactivity of a church
fellowship that fails to extend its love beyond itself?

Today, as always, young people want to know who
Jesus is. Each day, churches present images and examples
of Jesus to young people. Kids carefully examine the words,
plans, programs, activity or inactivity, and even pictures
on the wall to piece together an understanding of Jesus.

When I was in high school in the 1950s, Jesus was
not portrayed as a hard-working, mission-oriented champion of the faith. Church art and Sunday school material
pictured Jesus as a loving shepherd who tenderly held
little lambs in his soft, gentle hands. The pale and weak
portrayals of Jesus didn't make sense to me. I wondered
what had happened to the reality that Jesus was a carpenter. Surely he would be strong and have rough, calloused
hands. But I never saw a picture of Jesus looking like he
had just walked the rough, rugged roads of an arid, dusty
land.

The motion pictures in my mind featured Jesus living
for extended periods in the wilderness. He was probably
like John the Baptist, eating locusts with honey, munching
a few cactus blossoms for dessert, and then curling up in
the shelter of a rock or a tumbleweed to get a good
night's sleep. My image of Jesus pictured a man who
commanded the respect of fishermen. These wiry workers
wrestled with nets, worked in the wind and brushed sea
spray out of their eyes every day. But my image of Jesus
conflicted with the soft, pampered image portrayed in my
church.

My youth group reflected the same soft Jesus. We

played badminton and pingpong, ventured out for skating parties and hayrides with wiener roasts, and went to church camp in the summer. Mostly, we sat around and talked about the Bible. Sometimes, we leaped into action and got all sweaty playing softball. Then, we'd cool off with a refreshing plunge in the pool. My experience in the church's youth group just didn't match up with the picture of Jesus I saw in the New Testament.

Jesus commanded people to give, serve, feed, clothe, heal and take risks. Talk was not enough. All I experienced in church was talk and recreation. I enjoyed everything I did in the youth group, but the action seemed anemic, just like the pictures I saw on the wall.

Jesus taught by telling action-oriented stories. When someone asked him what the kingdom of God was like, he told a story about a woman working feverishly to clean her house when she lost a silver coin. She worked like a whirlwind until she found what she had lost. Then she called in all the neighbors to celebrate (Luke 15:8-9). I could understand and appreciate that simple story. But as I looked at fellowship dinners and choir cantatas as special occasions in the church, I still didn't see much that resembled the action of the Lord of Life. I didn't see the dynamic images of Jesus that leaped out at me from the pages of the New Testament.

I would have welcomed a chance to do something active, challenging and meaningful with my church youth group. It would have been refreshing to do something for someone else more than just passing the peas at a fellowship dinner. I would have loved to invite my friends to invest in the challenging experiences that grow out of a workcamp. We could have energized our faith by working together to improve significantly someone's home. But no one opened the door to service for our youth group.

Try to open the door to service for your youth group by planning a workcamp experience. Let's look at some key characteristics of workcamps to help you learn more about them.

Key Characteristics of Workcamps

Workcamps offer opportunities for young people to reach out and serve in Jesus' name. Workcamps give kids the chance to refurbish, refresh and renew run-down homes of low-income, elderly or needy people. Other characteristics of workcamps include:

1. Workcamps create an environment for developing Christian faith. A workcamp is like fertile soil where seeds can grow. Self-esteem is enhanced. Confidence builds. Enthusiasm for Christian service blossoms. And the Spirit of God flows through participants' serving hands, loving hearts and developing minds.

2. Workcamps focus on hard work. Young people expect to accomplish significant projects. Sponsors face many hours of tedious preparation. Planning groups nearly suffocate under the paper work involved in preparing and organizing. Participants may even suffer from a few blisters at the work site. Then, time must be set aside to prepare reports and establish post-workcamp strategies. But all your time and commitment will pay off when you see the Spirit of Jesus shining through the smiles of both residents and workers.

3. Workcamps shout "Action!" Christian love cascades through the hills and valleys of poverty areas; feelings of care and concern echo through the sound of pounding hammers.

A widow's loneliness fades as her home begins to shine with a new coat of paint. The hugs from her new friends on the work crew will warm her memories when winter storms swirl around her home.

4. Workcamps clearly enact the Good News that God gives his love freely. People who commit their energies to God's purposes become the channels for his action. These faithful instruments of God's love give themselves purely because God lives in them. The God of Abraham, Isaac and Jacob empowers them to go to new places and give a faithful witness of work. Reaching out to others is the most natural thing they can do.

5. Workcamps bring willing workers together to help needy people. Many young people discover what the kingdom of God is like as they work with completely new friends to repair and winterize someone else's house. They become united in their purpose. They learn to rely on one another. Together, they build a commitment to their mission.

Elderly couples, widows and widowers, low-income families, handicapped people and anyone who is lonely or forgotten welcome all the help they can get. And their homes scream for repair and rebuilding as the homes slowly wither and rot, unprotected from the ravages of wind, rain and sun.

One very old Blackfoot Indian on a reservation in Montana was invaded by six energetic, but somewhat nervous workcampers. The kids knew that the old gentleman had become depressed after his wife died three years earlier, and he had let the house fall into a shambles.

The work crew was assigned a list of tough projects for the week: painting inside and out, repairing broken windows and doors, rebuilding the back steps and putting a new roof on the house. With no time to lose, some of the girls began to clean the walls inside the house in preparation for some fresh paint. But when they opened the door to a back room, they discovered what must have been a three-year supply of clothes piled in huge stacks throughout the room. A slender pathway wound through the mountains of clothing. And the walls couldn't be painted until all the clothes were moved.

The group members decided that they would wash the old man's clothes in the kitchen sink. Then someone discovered an ancient washing machine under one of the mounds of clothes. Soon, clothes hung from every clothesline and fence in the yard.

By the end of the week, the crew members had a new friend they called "Gramps," and he had a huge smile on his face to go along with his rejuvenated house. When I visited the work site, the resident beamed with happiness as he bounced across the room to show me the closets full of freshly washed clothes. And he proudly told me that his new friends had taught him how to use the washer.

Perhaps his deep three-year-old pain healed a bit as the crew cranked up the washer that only his wife had used before. His clothes wouldn't create miniature mountains of smelly fabric again. Pride in his home returned with the invasion of the visitors who respectfully waded into the back rooms of his home. The kids were channels through which God's love flowed into this old man's life. Both he and his new friends would never again be the same.

Each of the crew members knew what it was like to find that "lost coin" in a house they had cleaned—and painted—and re-roofed—and repaired. Each of the workers felt a special glow inside, knowing that they had done something special for someone who clearly needed their help.

6. Workcamps give kids a feeling of accomplishment. Teenagers love to celebrate a truly significant accomplishment. They feel valuable and want to share that value with others. When they feel the wonderful power of helping someone else, they naturally want to keep using their new-found strength. So the workcamp experience lives on in the workcampers as they see themselves in a fresh, new, vital way as servants. They begin to believe they can make a real difference for someone else. And they discover some new strengths and abilities in the process.

Rita was one of the younger children in a large family. Her many sisters were hard-working, high achievers who almost fought to get to do the housework. Rita never lifted a finger around the house—she didn't have to. She grew up in a city and had no idea what life was like anywhere else. Then she went to a workcamp.

In the fast-moving responsibilities of a work crew, she proved she was a fast learner. The crew was assigned to paint a farmhouse owned by an aging couple. Rita pitched in with the daily farm chores as well as the assigned task of repairing the deteriorating home. She suddenly discovered the rigorous life of the farm and quickly grew to appreciate the hard work involved in growing crops and tending livestock.

Rita's experience opened her eyes to a whole new way of life. And she discovered a strength in herself that had been barricaded inside by the lack of opportunity to take on a difficult job.

Rita realized that her strength was part of God's self-giving love. She realized what it meant that Jesus had given himself so others could have life. She understood that sweat and hard work are parts of being a disciple of Jesus Christ.

7. Workcamps pave the pathway to service. Some young people are frustrated and feel like they are "dying on the vine" because of a lack of activity. Other young people realize that Christian faith demands a commitment to serve, but they have nowhere to go and nothing to do to show the power of God's love in their lives. Kids' atrophied muscles and spiritual strength can grow and harden as they apply their spirits and their flesh to God's work.

Jesus described his followers as active servants who love, feed, clothe and visit people in need. His words create nagging uneasiness in Christians who seldom serve or give of themselves. Some of us almost burst with the need to grab some kind of mission or ministry. We want to use the power God created in us. After taking in God's Word, we want to launch out from attending church services to putting Christ's love in action. A workcamp can be the vessel that takes us from preparation to performance.

8. Workcamps present a clear picture of the presence of God. God chooses to make himself known through the people who commit their lives to him. When our ideas and plans for service remain inside the walls of church buildings, we have little impact on people outside the church. But when the church sends a mission force of energetic workers into the homes of people who are lonely or in need, people start to notice God's action.

A tornado hit a large city in Texas several years ago. Many homes were destroyed. Many others were damaged. But the powerful funnels missed some homes completely, leaving little or no damage. One woman whose home was not hurt at all by the storm felt bypassed by the swarms of workers who were feverishly rebuilding the homes nearby. This lady's home was in desperate need, just from her lack of funds and her inability to do the work. She begged and pleaded for the disaster-recovery workers to do something for her. But state and federal guidelines prevented any work from being done on her home. During the year following the tornado, she became bitter and angry about the lack of response to her needs.

Some workcampers heard of her need and went to her home to help. They understood why she was so cranky and frowned so much. The signs of depression filled her home: clutter everywhere, layers of dirt on the floor, clothes piled on the furniture.

At first the woman complained constantly that the group was not working fast enough or doing things right. But as the work crew cleaned, repaired and painted the house, she gradually began to change. She quit complaining. She complimented the kids about their work. She even baked some cookies on the third day of the week. When visitors came to inspect the work, she bragged about "her" crew doing a fine job. She conducted tours around the house with people she wouldn't have let in her door just one week earlier. The local disaster-recovery people couldn't believe the change that had taken place in the previously crabby, angry old lady. But the crew members knew what had happened. They had experienced her change and knew the One who got things going.

9. Workcamps give young people an opportunity to talk about their faith. When workers arrive at a site, the residents can't hold back their curiosity and, sometimes, suspicion. They want to know what has motivated these young people to come work on their homes.

Residents are carefully assured that there will be no charge for the work. But some fear that hidden costs will spring up after the job is done. In nearly every case, residents question the young workers about why they are there. "Who's paying these kids to do all this work?" they want to know.

And it's fun to watch the teenagers grin and say: "No one. We earned the money to pay for the chance to come here and work." Surprised looks from old ladies, hard-nosed businessmen and agency coordinators should be captured on film. The caption could be: "One hundred ways to show disbelief."

Some people insist the young people are work-release inmates from a detention home. Others question their sanity. Most just grin back and ask for the rest of the punch line, since they know "the youngsters" are joking. Everyone knows that no one would voluntarily pay to get filthy, sweaty and tired working on someone else's home.

A few people catch on quickly: "They're Christian kids, aren't they?" The Bible readers and lifelong Christians recognize the mark of the Master in the self-giving effort to serve without thought for payment. And when these people realize they have guessed right, a special glow radiates from their faces as they anticipate becoming one in spirit with God's servants.

Enthusiastic work crews always manage to convince even the skeptical residents that they are not being paid to work. The skeptics' curiosity then opens another door. "Well, why *are* you here then?" It's always fun to hear the young people explain to the baffled residents that they are Christian and feel a need to use some of their strength and abilities to help with needed repairs. The more theologically astute crew members usually point out that God's love came to them as a gift and that their families and their church now have sent them to share the gift. They feel a certain need to give because they now are part of the gift: God's love in Jesus Christ.

Careful and consistent explaining will clear up the confused perceptions of Christianity that have lurked for years in the shadows of the minds of many people. The Good News about God's love is so unbelievable to so many people that it needs to be acted out. The free help that workcamps bring to people clarifies God's gift of love. No longer do these needy people feel bypassed in life. They know Someone cares.

10. Workcamps open a channel of outpouring love that completes in us our need to give. If I could draw a cartoon about the tragedy of today's church, I would sketch a person being filled with living water—like a balloon being filled by a garden hose—until little tiny streams of water begin spurting out of pinholes, relieving the pressure just enough to keep the balloon from bursting. For too many Christians, small acts of kindness relieve the pressing need to serve someone significantly. When this happens to us, we risk becoming like the Dead Sea. Blessings come in and nothing goes out. Through workcamps, we finally can complete the Christian cycle of giving because we have received.

Christians need action in order to be healthy. Love flowing through the arms and legs of servant-workers prevents the gangrene of apathy and inactivity. Young people who want to serve others now simply echo the natural need of Christians to "be about the Lord's business."

The natural need to give of themselves propels youth groups toward workcamps. Youthful Christians feel they have a lot to prove. They want to show that they can do important jobs. They want to explode in the world with action. They want to silence the imposing advice of older people to "wait their turn." They want to make a difference in the lives of people around them.

Workcamps flourish with opportunities to make a dynamic statement about the value of young Christians as active workers in the church. Teenagers want and need to do something truly meaningful and important in the lives of others.

Typical comments are heard in every workcamp. "I didn't know so many kids went to church. I'm not embarrassed to be a Christian anymore." "I only wish I could take this feeling home with me and live it every day." "It's exciting to see so many kids showing their faith and the power of Jesus' love in their lives."

Although a workcamp focuses not on evangelism but on mission and service, tremendous awareness of the Gospel takes place as the workers live out the commandments of Jesus. They feel what it's like to love their neighbor and to sacrifice a big part of themselves so others might have life. They become new creatures daily. They live in the power and presence of Christ.

The special release of God's love in the actions of the workers leaves a powerful impression on the people they serve. Residents may be very shy at the beginning of the week. But the compelling love being shown in action tugs at their hearts until they respond in some way to the crew.

Some residents try to give gifts to the workers. It's hard to turn down someone's gift, but it's also hard to accept a gift from someone who has almost nothing to begin with.

Many issues are raised. Creative responses tumble out as the week progresses. Cookies and cakes, iced tea and Coke, banjo concerts and unaccompanied solos all express the residents' acceptance of the gift of love that has spread throughout their homes.

Departing creates its own memories. Tears flow as the group prepares to leave. Smiles and promises to write nearly overwhelm the work site. And the workers begin to realize the impact they have had on the people who will never forget their smiling faces, bleeding fingers and bruised shins. Although much has been shared, there is also a sense of loss as the mission draws to a close.

Local newspaper, radio and TV representatives often get caught up in the uniqueness of self-giving workers.

Even the most hard-nosed reporters become fascinated by young people working for a week with old folks and low-income people. They become amazed when they hear that the young people are *paying* to work.

One TV reporter in Mobile, Alabama, asked a teenager from Minnesota: "Why are you here? Why have you journeyed all the way from Minnesota and paid a fee to get to work on these homes?"

The young man looked directly into the camera and replied: "I'm here because of Jesus. I'm working for Jesus."

The reporter couldn't compute what he said at first. "Oh?" Then it hit who Jesus was. "Oh! Now I understand. You're Christians. That's why you work and who you work for."

The message of Christian service is so unusual that it startles people. The Christian service the kids provide sharply contrasts with the bad news about teenagers that is often spread by the media. Through workcamps, reporters gain a refreshing opportunity to print and report the positive side of the new generation.

When the reports hit the community, people will begin to recycle the question, "What makes young people pay to do all this work?" Then, local churches will be able to preach the Good News of Jesus Christ to answer those recurring questions.

Chapter Two

The Benefits of Workcamps

The first chapter highlighted the key characteristics and values of workcamping. Now let's look more closely at how workcamps benefit young people, youth groups, residents, communities and churches. While planning a workcamp trip, you'll need to explain the benefits in detail to your group, to the kids' parents and to the church leaders.

Benefits to Young People

Workcamps offer many valuable experiences to the young people who participate in them. Following are several benefits that kids receive from a workcamp:

1. Young people develop spiritual insight through their new experiences at workcamps. They begin to see life in a new, Christian way. A young person who often complained that his friends lived in nicer houses than he did attended a summer workcamp. After four days of working in a poverty area, he reported to the rest of the workcampers that for the first time, he saw how much he really was thankful for. He discovered many happy people who owned practically nothing. "I'm totally ashamed at the way I've been feeling about my home," he confessed. "I'm going to appreciate things a lot more when I go back."

This young man had taken a step toward becoming the "new creation" that the Apostle Paul talked about. "Therefore, if anyone is in Christ, he is a new creation;

the old has gone, the new has come" (2 Corinthians 5:17). The workcamper was beginning to see his home and family through the eyes of Christ. A new appreciation burst into his mind. He identified himself as someone with special opportunities, blessings and gifts.

The workcamp experience helped another young person change the way he saw himself. Ted was smaller than other guys his age. He had been born with a crippled leg and a clubfoot. Surgery had straightened his leg but had not totally eliminated the clubfoot. Unless you saw Ted in shorts and barefoot, you wouldn't suspect any problem. But Ted always wore long pants, and never went without shoes.

Since everyone wore shorts during the hot part of the day, the crew members teased Ted unmercifully for wearing long pants. He dodged their taunts with sly responses and avoided the expected humiliation . . . until the group suddenly decided to go for a swim.

After pumping up his courage, Ted finally suited up and plunged into the pool. He was greeted with rousing applause and cheers for wearing his swimsuit. Then, one by one, the group members began to notice that Ted was an excellent swimmer. He had spent many hours swimming for therapy and had even polished his diving skills. After a few superior dives, Ted was a celebrity in the group.

Later in the week, Ted surprised everyone during an evening discussion. He voiced his astonishment that no one had said anything about his foot. Hesitantly, he pulled back his pants and took off his shoe so the others could see why he never wore shorts. He sheepishly confessed that he had wanted to share his swimming and diving ability, but felt too embarrassed to wear a swimsuit in front of other people. He nearly cried as he told how the group's acceptance had overpowered his self-consciousness.

By taking a risk and showing the part of himself that he thought was unacceptable, Ted felt a new confidence that freed him to just be himself in the group. When he finished his short speech, he sighed with relief. Suddenly, he pulled out a pair of scissors and a pair of long pants. With great flourish, Ted slashed the legs off the pants and created a pair of shorts. The group members shouted their approval and lifted him on their shoulders like a champion. Ted, too, began seeing himself in a new way. He understood the way others saw him through God's eyes.

2. God gives a special power to people who serve actively in his name. Feeling that power imprints the spirit of God's love on the hearts of many young people. In some mysterious and wondrous way, the positive response to Jesus' call to serve implants in a person the power and perspective of the new creation. This personal experience of self-giving love can shock a person into a new way of life.

Pam, a high school senior from Pennsylvania, attended a workcamp in the Appalachian Mountains. She signed up for the workcamp mostly because her mother insisted that she try it out. Pam had been in a lot of trouble. Her reputation was shot. But the group encouraged her to forget her past and dive into the workcamp activities.

The new challenges of the work projects captivated Pam's interest. Her work crew faced one of the toughest projects at the workcamp. But they attacked the crumbling old home with new boards and fresh paint. The residents were nearly overwhelmed with all the activity around the house. They told everyone how wonderful the young people were. The more the old couple bragged, the harder the crew worked and the more they accomplished. By the end of the week, the kids' faces glowed with satisfaction. They beamed with a deep inner awareness that they had done something wonderful for the aging homeowners.

Pam felt exhilarated. She blurted out her story to her mother the minute she arrived back home. Drugs had never given her this tremendously uplifting feeling. Her many boyfriends hadn't made her feel so completely loved. Her wild partying hadn't made her happy. But the Spirit of God working through her to help that little old couple in the mountains had completely filled her with both peace and excitement. She knew she could be someone valuable and important. She was becoming happy with life.

Pam discovered the presence of God within herself. She experienced the power of doing God's work with others. She caught the excitement of Christian service. God's love and acceptance were powerfully present in the very real and very active work crew. Pam felt new worth in herself—the worth of a new creation.

3. Young people learn the process of Christian growth. The New Testament clearly presents Jesus as someone who helps and serves others. By following his model, we discover how to become new creatures of God. Young people feel God's presence when they reach out to help others. This awareness of God's presence stimulates growth. Young people begin to look for ways to take risks for others. During this process, they discover the new creation in themselves.

Chris, a younger member of his youth group, felt inferior because his family wasn't financially well off. His experience at a workcamp showed him that he had some "currency" even more valuable than money. He learned to give time and skills to people who valued what he was offering. His efforts uncovered the value and importance of his abilities. He'll never feel "poor" again. His currency accrues interest every time he helps someone.

4. Young people develop personal relationships in a workcamp through openness and sharing. Kids naturally talk about the new experiences of each day. They reflect on their experiences, thoughts and feelings and try to make sense out of the newness of workcamping. Applying the insights of scripture to the daily struggles with the work projects paints a wider picture of what life is about.

The members of one work crew suddenly felt surprised by all the work they did. They began to question why they had done so much hard work for a stranger.

They finally decided that helping had just seemed like a "rule" made by church leaders. This rule seemed abstract and frightening. At the workcamp, they had a chance actually to be helpful. For the first time, the kids realized that they were an important part of something big and necessary.

One skinny little guy said: "I never knew getting dirty could be fun. I've even been able to make big changes in someone's home. Those people were really happy that our crew came to work at their place."

5. When young people become aware of their value and importance, they feel free to use their abilities in new ways. Kids discover a new way of seeing themselves. They begin to understand how their life can be a gift to someone else. They find new ways to serve God.

Challenges abound at a workcamp. Everyone learns new skills. For those who are novices, there are simple jobs like hammering and painting. Every job makes a big difference when carefully applied to a home. Some tasks, like underpinning, are completely different from anything kids have seen back home. And digging an outhouse pit is usually a new skill for the majority of workers.

Many of the houses create unusual challenges that even the most experienced carpenters have never faced before:

- living quarters actually pieced together out of available material;
- trailers added to shacks;
- lean-tos added to log houses;
- ceilings constructed at different heights;
- floors made of the dirt beneath the house;
- bridges built across streams;
- walls constructed in a creek bed; and
- hexagonal homes made of mud and logs. Everyone learns new skills working with the ancient architecture of the hogans in the Navajo Nation communities.

6. Pride of workmanship grows as workcampers

watch their projects take shape. In most areas, crews must produce high-quality results, since inspectors will visit each site to assure that the work is completed according to established standards.

Returning workcampers often develop so much self-confidence that they feel like tackling any project they see. One crew of roofers faced a particularly challenging project: a house with several rotten boards under some old, weathered shingles.

Freddie, a thin, wiry workcamper from Dallas, sounded like a chamber of commerce public relations director describing what his crew from the past year did on a similar project. He completely, carefully and proudly outlined all the ingenious plans his previous crew had devised for patching the old roof.

The crew of workers followed Freddie's energetic leadership. When I returned to the site at the end of the week, the roof looked wonderful. Freddie beamed as he related the many challenges they had faced in trying to complete the project. He would be telling workcamp stories for months after returning home.

7. All kinds of young people grow through their workcamp experience. Well-planned workcamps automatically challenge people with negative attitudes or lack of confidence. They launch people into experiences completely different from their usual lifestyles.

Phyllis didn't care much for Bible study or servanthood. Her strict parents had drilled into her that she was not ready to do anything important. Phyllis believed she should just wait until she grew up to attempt anything of consequence. She seemed content to sit back and do nothing in the youth group. So no one was surprised that she gave little help in planning and preparing for the trip to the work area.

At the workcamp, though, Phyllis was forced to carry specific responsibilities because of the organized approach of the work crew. She cooked. She assisted another worker who sprained his ankle. She planned group discussions for the end of the workday.

Phyllis learned about service and what she was like as a servant. After the workcamp, Phyllis told her youth group how one of the Bible discussions really helped her. Her crew had studied 1 Peter 4:10-11: "Each one should use whatever gift he has received to serve others, faithfully administering God's grace in its various forms. If anyone speaks, he should do it as one speaking the very words of God. If anyone serves, he should do it with the strength God provides, so that in all things God may be praised through Jesus Christ." Phyllis said: "The most important thing I learned at the workcamp was that no matter who you are, God has something for you to do. He will give you the strength you need to do it."

Challenging responsibilities leave no doubt in a teen-ager's mind that he or she can accomplish important tasks. A new sense of personal value erupts in the minds of those who have accomplished something they know is im-portant to someone else.

Decision-making opportunities thrust young people into a new awareness of their ability to carry responsibility for important jobs. Some decisions must be made immedi-ately. If it is about to rain, there isn't time to wait for someone else to decide to cover the roof with plastic so water won't ruin the ceilings inside. All the crews must de-cide when to stop for a break, how much additional material they will need to finish the project, and what to do when a resident asks for more work to be done than was originally planned.

Girls carry equal responsibility for all jobs on the work crew. No one expects them to sit back and watch the guys work. Sometimes even the residents have to be shown that girls, as well as guys, can pitch in and help with major projects.

Susan, a senior who was preparing for college, saw her workcamp experience as training for going to a new campus and making new friends. She learned to talk with people she had just met and began to develop friendships.

She learned to work with people by doing whatever was
necessary. Her confidence grew tremendously in the pressure of completing a project in just one week. She left the
workcamp with a positive and confident outlook for
college.

   **8. Experiencing new cultures helps kids under-
stand people and traditions that differ from their
own.** As groups travel to various areas of the country,
they discover that their way of doing things is not the
only way.

   Kids acquire new tastes for different foods—or rein-
force a liking for the food back home. Navajo tacos, grits,
alligator-tail chili, mutton stew, sweetened ice tea and fried
okra are examples of conversation pieces on the dinner
table at a workcamp. Discovering what other people like
to eat leads to more complete understanding of the life of
a given area. Stereotypes shatter as kids realize that people
don't fit the preconceptions of their area of the country or
their circumstance in life.

   A workcamp in Chester, Pennsylvania, opened the
eyes of many young people who had never experienced
friendship within urban, black neighborhoods. A workcamp in the Navajo Nation in Arizona led many teenagers
to a deeper understanding of people who seem shy, but
quickly become friendly when you enter their homes. A
workcamp in Mexico helped teenagers realize the differences in cultures as they wore long pants and long-sleeve
shirts in 100-degree heat.

   Understanding other people and other cultures leads
workcampers and residents into opportunities to grow. As-
sumed perceptions and ways of doing things are challenged and even changed. Love develops during a
workweek and opens the door to understanding and acceptance.

   Many groups use a workcamp trip as an opportunity
to venture into new environments. One group visited New
Orleans on the way to Florida and ate at a fancy French
restaurant. The young people rehearsed and polished their

social skills before they went so the waiters wouldn't crack up while serving their table.

9. Large workcamps that draw from many different Christian denominations help kids see similarities of their faith. Workcampers of various denominations talk and work together. Kids meet people who have the same basic faith, even though the ways they practice that faith may differ. A sense of cooperation grows as people from many different backgrounds work together.

It's fun to see how various groups accommodate each other's different beliefs by respecting the other's right not to be forced into anything it doesn't want to do. Consideration for others grows as love becomes more powerful within the workcamp.

Benefits to a Youth Group

Workcamps offer many valuable experiences to kids individually as well as to youth groups. Let's look at several benefits for youth groups who participate in workcamps:

1. A sense of community builds within a youth group as members plan and work toward a common purpose. Workcamping challenges groups with a complex project that takes much work and preparation. As the group shares responsibilities, mutual reliance on one another builds trust and respect. Even solving problems together helps the group feel closer as it painstakingly makes plans and overcomes obstacles.

Each step taken toward a successful workcamp builds confidence and satisfaction within the group. As young people work together toward a common goal, the investment of time and energy forms a bond of friendship.

Training for work skills also creates an environment for enriching the sense of community within the group. As individuals struggle with learning and improving new skills, the group draws closer together. Members feel a special camaraderie through experiencing the learning process together.

2. Traveling to workcamps sparks Christian growth. If a group ventures beyond its local area to a workcamp, the time and effort shared together in travel create opportunities for Christian growth within the group. Kids serve one another by taking responsibility for cleaning and maintaining vehicles, cooking meals (if the group does any camping), leading devotions and discussions, and even forgiving each other's transgressions.

3. Tackling work projects challenges youth groups to develop strengths and interdependence. Kids begin to stretch their trust and commitment. Each person must grow and learn new skills. Everyone must do his or her part to push the work along. In the process, each person discovers the value of other people in completing a big job.

4. Workcamping creates unique opportunities for evangelism. The youth group will appeal to more kids outside the group. Action, adventure and achievement will captivate an interest in Christ from young people who previously were not interested in a church group.

The excitement of the youth group members about the workcamp becomes contagious and infects their friends with curiosity. The work itself intrigues young people outside the group who want to accomplish something with obvious meaning and purpose. Young men often want to use their strength and develop skills with home repair. Young women often want to show they can work hard and accomplish important tasks.

When a group returns from a workcamp, its effervescence naturally attracts others who will want to get involved the next time around.

5. Youth group kids can influence their family members toward Christian growth. Young people who invest themselves in a workcamp can create repercussions within their families. Doug and his family started attending church just a few weeks before the workcamp trip. The youth advisers invited him to go along with the group. Af-

ter a little uncertainty and some encouragement from youth group members, Doug finally agreed to go. He was a chubby little guy and not very outgoing. He also had a laugh that was both unique and irritating.

During the workcamp, one of the kids finally told Doug that he had a strange laugh. Doug was offended at first, since some of the group members started to imitate his laugh in horrible ways. Then everyone's laugh was examined and imitated.

Doug proved to be the best mimic in the group. Soon he was able to reproduce almost every laugh. His favorite trick was to sneak up behind someone and imitate his or her laugh, trying to confuse the rest of the group and the victim at the same time.

The group's experience with laughter styles opened the way to a Bible study focusing on varieties of gifts within a church. The group scrutinized the whole matter of different people and different laughs. One boy said that he didn't think it was fair to make fun of Doug because of his laugh. This boy had a distinct Boston accent and knew what it was like to be teased for something that wasn't easy to control. The group members reacted by expressing their appreciation for Doug's many other qualities and gifts. Doug soon felt a part of the group and began to make significant contributions toward positive attitudes within the group.

Later, when Doug's family wanted to try different churches before committing to one, he told them he didn't need to shop around. He knew he was accepted and had found a church home right where he was. The next week, the whole family joined the church.

6. A workcamp experience creates opportunities to include more young people in the group. The bigger the work project, the more workers will be needed. There will be many different roles, responsibilities and jobs to perform. As more people get involved, more options will be available to choose the right person for a particular task. The expanded responsibilities that are necessary for workcamps create needs for more people. And more people will feel needed.

7. Youth groups will become aware of the need for committed Christian workers throughout the nation. Group members will personally experience the needs of hungry, disadvantaged or bypassed people. Reaching out to help others will no longer be abstract and philosophical. Kids will remember flesh-and-blood examples of people who need God's love. They'll experience the conditions that make some people need the helping hands of Christ's followers.

As young people see each other making a difference in someone else's life, they'll also realize how valuable their friends are. It will be harder to make fun of someone who has just repaired a roof and built new steps for a crippled little old lady. Each member of the group will be seen as an important part of the active love of God. The power of that realization will have a lasting effect, which may extend well beyond the youth group.

The members of one work crew had impressed a whole neighborhood by the time they had completed their project. They worked all week on a house while the owner lay in the hospital in the final stages of a terminal illness. The situation was unusual: The owner had no family who could refurbish her home to get it ready to be sold. She desperately needed money to pay hospital bills, and she worried about her funeral expenses. The crew managed a minor miracle in completely repairing and painting the house, cleaning the yard and trimming the shrubs and hedges.

The workcampers never met the lady, and she saw only a snapshot of what they had done. Because of the crew's work, she was able to sell her house. She then put her affairs in order, and lived her last days with a peace that she wouldn't have enjoyed if the workcamp hadn't come along.

This crew learned an important Christian truth. You don't need to see or know people in order to love them and touch their lives in an important way. During the first day, these workers noticed neighbors peering at them from behind curtains, and then from porches, and finally from the sidewalk in front of the house. The neighbors were curious and had many questions. Why would a bunch of teenagers work that hard to fix the old lady's house? They couldn't believe the youth didn't know the lady, and that they were working at no cost! By the evening of the first day, the workcampers had just about convinced the cynical neighbors of their good intentions.

The next day, as the youth group returned and worked again in the hot sun, the neighbors brought jugs of cold drinks as a gesture of friendship. That night, the young people struggled to understand why people couldn't believe they were paying to work for someone they didn't know. They caught another glimpse of the unique Christian belief that calls us to love, simply because God has already loved us.

Benefits to Residents and Communities

Residents and communities gain many unforgettable memories as well as invaluable improvements on their homes. Following are several benefits workcamps give to residents and communities:

1. Residents enjoy warmer, safer and more attractive housing. Rotten boards are ripped out and replaced with strong, safe lumber. Cracks and crevices are caulked or stuffed with insulation. Roofs are repaired and re-covered so damaging moisture doesn't wander inside. Residents benefit from a warmer, more economical home as heat loss is reduced.

A new coat of paint spread across a weathered wall lifts a homeowner's attitude. And if the workers happen to be smiling, exuberant, friendly teenagers, the homeowner will be overcome by friendship and joy within a week.

One woman in West Virginia hid in her bedroom when the work crew first arrived. She didn't emerge from her sanctuary until the second day—after her brother coaxed her out of her room.

By the week's end, the kids had found a way into her heart. She was smiling and serving cookies she had baked the night before. She joined in the morning discussion of scripture. And she nearly warped the floor with her tears as the crew packed up to leave. The group had been the bright spot of her summer. She rediscovered her ability to be sociable and friendly. Her brother, too, was overjoyed that the crew had helped her break out of her self-imposed shell.

2. Workcampers and residents contribute to each other's lives. One of the most powerful experiences I have seen happened at a workcamp in Tennessee. An older couple's home was literally falling down around them. The husband had built the house himself. But 50 years of buffeting by wind and rain had nearly turned the house into a fragile, unstable shack.

Several workcamps were planned in a series of weeks to build a completely new home beside the old one. When our workcamp started in the first week of August, the couple's new home was almost complete. Our crew applied fresh paint inside and out, put the finishing touches on the house, and then moved the old furniture from the crumbling shack to the new house.

The husband had a difficult time while the work crews labored during the summer. His wife confided that he had grown bitter toward God years ago when a car wreck killed their son. The husband rejected the church, where he had been an elder, and refused even to pray at the dinner table. His wife had remained faithful in the hope that he would return to his Christian way of life.

At first he ignored the groups working diligently on his property. But as the summer progressed, he became more open to the young people. When our crew members finished moving all the furniture, they decided to have a dedication ceremony on the last day of the workcamp. While the workcampers were singing a hymn, the bitter, old mountaineer began to sing. His wife nearly collapsed with surprise! Then, as prayers were being offered for God's blessing on the new home, the old man offered a prayer that God would accept him once again into his family. Everyone was in tears, and his wife sang a special song of praise to God for the presence of the young Christian witnesses who had worked their way into her husband's heart.

These examples represent the personal, spiritual element of the interaction between workcampers and residents. Each situation is different. Each opportunity to be part of someone else's life is unique. But both the residents and the workcampers enjoy the chance to contribute to each other's lives.

3. Community agencies and local mission organizations receive valuable assistance in meeting their annual service goals. Many agencies struggle under a huge backlog of projects they could never complete. More applications for aid arrive daily, and their crews just can't catch up.

Typically, local workers in the community stay close to their main office, since travel to areas farther away would take valuable time. They are most efficient when they stay close to their warehouse where they can complete more projects. Workcamps can establish a base of operations near the outlying projects and help agencies catch up with projects they couldn't otherwise accomplish. Flexibility with arrangements allows workcamps to serve the needs of people who live in remote areas.

Many mission organizations desperately need materials. These groups usually have strong commitments to serve, but little cash to spend on projects. Workcamps can help most by bringing in cash and materials to accomplish projects that would otherwise be impossible.

4. Adventurous groups can be tremendously effective with inner-city workcamps. Huge problems with run-down housing scream for attention. Inner-city mission organizations desperately need help. The benefits go beyond the physical repairs to homes. People living in poor housing areas receive a personal boost knowing that someone cares and understands. Personal attention along with significant effort to improve living conditions are extremely helpful and meaningful.

5. Agency or mission workers in depressed areas often need extra help. Jobs in depressed areas tie the agency workers to sometimes insurmountable problems that have been around for generations. Seeing their efforts swallowed up in a sea of difficulties can leave workers depressed and apathetic. Enthusiastic workcampers can help lift their spirits, at least for a while. Returning groups can be a beacon of hope throughout the year.

6. Residents develop new pride and a willingness to work to improve their own surroundings. Workcamps are often held in areas that are depressed both economically *and* psychologically. A loss of hope pervades. When energetic workcampers enter the area, a new sense of hope and pride begins lifting the residents' spirits. At first, residents may peer suspiciously at the workcampers. They often call or visit the resident receiving the assistance to find out what in the world is going on.

But after watching the workcampers a couple of days, many neighbors begin working on their own homes, cleaning up the yard, trimming the shrubs, etc. Workcampers are the catalyst to renewed hope and pride in the area.

Benefits to the Church

Young people, youth groups, residents and communities receive valuable experiences and memories from workcamps—and so does the church. Following are several workcamp benefits for the church:

1. The church gains a deeper sense of mission. The activities and presentations of the young people will place the servant theme in the forefront of people's thoughts. (The activities and presentations will be described later in this book.) This "selling" approach to the general membership focuses attention on the purpose and value of Christian servanthood. Unless the church believes in its mission to serve as followers of Jesus, the membership will not accept workcamp ministry. But the process of accepting a workcamp will jostle the souls of the members until they make some decision about the appropriateness of the mission of workcamping. The struggle itself will lead to deeper commitment for many people in the church.

2. The church defines more clearly the level of activity it expects young people to take within the church family. Through a workcamp, the church can express trust in young people as its designated representatives. Teenagers will be seen as facilitators of the church's mission. If church leaders commit support and finances to the mission of the youth group, they will be endorsing the youth group members as viable missionaries of the church. Adults will recognize young people as capable members who can articulate the purpose of the church. Adults will support specific efforts to put that purpose into action.

The impact of a workcamp will influence church life for many years, as it draws upon the leadership abilities of those who have sharpened their commitment by serving others.

3. The entire church models a commitment to service. Young people will recognize and appreciate that commitment. As they see the adults financially supporting the youth group project, they'll learn the value of supporting representatives of the church. This process will help build a tradition of mission as a high priority in the life of the church. Workcamping will be a clearly identifiable mission experience taking its place in the significant activities of the total church program.

The youth group's workcamp effort will plant the idea of personal service in the minds of all members. Everyone will be involved to some degree in the initial decision to approve the youth group's request to tackle a workcamp.

Further involvement will grow through funding the work-camp. The church will be involved in its financial under-girding whether the workcamp becomes an item in the general budget, grows out of the youth department budget or is totally funded by the youth group with fund-raising efforts.

4. Adults who attend the workcamp as sponsors become advocates of servant projects within the church. These adults will know the power of reaching out in God's love and experience the power of that love. Many times, these adults recruit other adults into a work-camp experience—locally, nationally and worldwide.

As adults become more involved in mission-oriented activities, the whole church experiences spiritual growth. The cycle of outreach will become a part of the church's lifestyle. The fear of committing to new outreach missions under God's guidance will diminish. Each person will come to know that he or she can make a difference by working to create the vision of Christ's presence in the lives of people who need God's love.

A workcamp will powerfully affect the life of a local congregation. Church members will hear the call to mis-sion. They will see the effects of responding to that call as they watch and hear the young people share their ex-periences and reactions.

The power of God's love will flow through the church in a special way as young people share their dis-coveries and anticipate new opportunities to serve. The church will celebrate its opportunities to serve as followers of the One who gave himself so that all people might live in the fullness of God's presence.

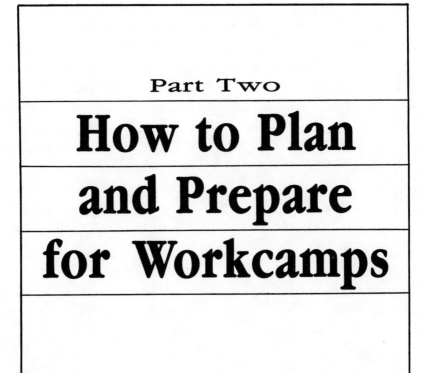

Part Two

How to Plan and Prepare for Workcamps

Chapter Three
Initial Decisions

Before diving into the details of planning a workcamp, you must know whether the pastor and other church leaders will support it. One youth leader planned a Mexico workcamp with his kids, stirring up their enthusiasm about the servanthood project. When the senior pastor found out, he cancelled the trip due to fears of taking the kids to another country. All the plans were wasted, and the kids' enthusiasm was crushed.

Avoid this situation by telling church leaders you are interested in planning a workcamp experience for the youth group. Once they know about your idea and give you their support, then begin assessing the readiness of the kids and the church.

Assessing Readiness

Workcamping launches a group into exciting Christian growth; however, the demands on a youth group also can erupt into gigantic problems, tearing apart groups that are not ready for the workcamp experience.

Some groups begin their project only to discover they are not ready to invest the time and energy necessary to make a workcamp successful. Careful assessment of your kids' spiritual, emotional and physical maturity will help you decide if they are ready for the opportunities and risks of a major mission.

Your church should also be ready for an outpouring of its resources through the youth group. Church members will need to understand the mission of service and self-giving that will encompass your group. Church leaders should prepare to support the group's efforts. The young people will face the responsibility of explaining the purpose of the workcamp to the congregation members and answering their questions. The church leaders' support and encouragement will be crucial as the youth group seeks official approval.

Use Chart 1 as a guide to evaluate your youth group's readiness for a workcamp. Ask a few adult leaders to help with the evaluation. Remind them that the information must remain confidential, since personalities are involved. Have the adult leaders individually fill out the forms for each group member. Then meet and share the results.

Another alternative is to let kids evaluate themselves. Let everyone examine his or her own level of maturity, experience, work skills, and spiritual and physical readiness to determine areas of strength and areas that need improvement. These results will not be shared, but used for personal reflection. If you use this approach, simplify the form by deleting spaces for names of all the kids. Each person will evaluate only himself or herself, not the others.

Use the numerical ratings as general guidelines, not as the final authority. The numerical scales provide helpful information as you evaluate certain factors.

Once the youth group has been evaluated, list the strengths and weaknesses on a sheet of newsprint. Compose goals for the group in light of this list, highlighting strengths and trying to improve on weaknesses.

Use Chart 2 to assess your church's readiness for the project. Find out whether you have the necessary resources to plan a workcamp. You may need to ask other church leaders who have a clearer perspective of some specific groups in the church to help with this appraisal.

After you have completed the first two assessment forms, use Chart 3 to evaluate your group's overall needs.

As you consider conducting a workcamp, think about God's will for your youth group. Remember, God empowers the church to love and serve. These fruits of the Christian life insist that we help disadvantaged people. People

Chart 1
Readiness Appraisal Form

This appraisal will let you know areas of strength in your group and areas that need improvement. Fill in names, or code the names by number if you want the results to be presented to the group anonymously. Evaluate your impressions of each person for each area by using the following scale:

1 = Help!　　　　3 = Average　　　5 = Excellent
2 = Needs improvement　4 = Very good

Name	Maturity	Experience	Work Skills	Spiritually Ready	Physically Ready	Overall Score
1.						
2.						
3.						
4.						
5.						
6.						
7.						
8.						
9.						

Composite Score

Add the scores for each column, then divide by the number of people listed. You will then have a composite score for each area for the total group. Add the scores across the page for each person for each area, then divide by five to obtain the average score for each person.

Once you fill out an appraisal form for each person, ask yourself these questions:
● Is anyone obviously unprepared in most areas to handle a workcamp?
● Is anyone borderline or questionable in one or more areas?
● Do the people with strengths in the group balance with those who need to improve?
● Will there be adequate support for those who need to improve?
● What areas need improvement for the group as a whole?
● How much work will it take for the group to strengthen those areas?
● What are the areas of strength for the total group?
● How will those areas benefit the group in preparing for and functioning in a workcamp?
● Overall, how do I feel about the group's ability to handle a workcamp?

Permission to photocopy this chart granted for local church use only. Copyright © 1987 by Group Books, Inc., Box 481, Loveland, CO 80539.

experience the fruits of love and service when they participate in servanthood ministries for the church. Jesus calls
us to serve in his name, and he works in us as we perform
in self-giving service. This infusion of Christ's Spirit happens naturally in a workcamp environment.

Maturing Christian young people understand that a

Chart 2
Functional Appraisal Form

Evaluate your youth group and congregation on functional readiness for a workcamp. Find out if you have the necessary resources to
make a workcamp successful. Use the following scale:
1 = Help!
2 = Needs improvement
3 = Average
4 = Very good
5 = Excellent

1. Ability to raise adequate funds: 1 2 3 4 5

2. Travel resources available: 1 2 3 4 5

3. Appropriate adult leadership available: 1 2 3 4 5

4. Capable leadership within youth group: 1 2 3 4 5

5. Youth group understands and accepts servant role: 1 2 3 4 5

6. Group has time and ability to do major planning: 1 2 3 4 5

7. Fund raising can fit into youth program: 1 2 3 4 5

8. Positive support expected from parents: 1 2 3 4 5

9. Positive support expected from congregation: 1 2 3 4 5

10. Positive support expected from church staff: 1 2 3 4 5

After you rate each area, ask yourself these questions:
● What are the areas of major concern?
● What strengths stand out?
● What further information do I need to make this evaluation?
● Overall, how do I feel about the youth group's and church's
readiness for a workcamp?

Permission to photocopy this chart granted for local church use only. Copyright © 1987 by
Group Books, Inc., Box 481, Loveland, CO 80539.

workcamp can never be simply a week of work and activity. Christian mission always reaches beyond mere work to an outpouring of love. But surprisingly, this outpouring flows both ways. As Christ reaches out from workcampers toward people in need, he personally fills the workcampers' lives with his Spirit.

Young people reaching out in workcamps grow in their ability to see the long-range impact of a workcamp. They realize their efforts during the workweek will be remembered for many years. They understand that they will help open many hearts and minds to the Christian message.

Maturity enables a young person to commit to a long period of preparation. Workcamps demand careful and tedious planning, and extraordinary advance effort. Only mature young people will hold on to distant goals for many months while they are raising funds in the dead of winter.

Chart 3
Group Needs Assessment

After you have filled out the readiness and functional appraisal forms, use this form to assess overall needs of your youth group. Use this scale:

1 = Help!
2 = Needs improvement
3 = Average
4 = Very good
5 = Excellent

1. Christian education and instruction in basic beliefs: 1 2 3 4 5

2. Spiritual enrichment: 1 2 3 4 5

3. Service and outreach: 1 2 3 4 5

4. Evangelism—increase in number of members: 1 2 3 4 5

Other considerations:

Permission to photocopy this chart granted for local church use only. Copyright © 1987 by Group Books, Inc., Box 481, Loveland, CO 80539.

Mature young people also see a workcamp's long-range impact. They recognize the importance of planting seeds that may not sprout while they are at the workcamp. This mature perspective leads them to invest in future possibilities without immediate personal gratification.

Each person's stamina will be tested. A workcamp requires concentrating on a specific job for a full week. Many crews work tediously for three days just to lay foundations for the last two days. Then they see a dramatic change in the project. These delays challenge young people to believe in the week's goal. Work projects also promote patience, since daily progress may not be clearly visible.

Your group members will appreciate opportunities to discuss their readiness for service projects. They'll want to know just how ready they are for a challenge. Schedule several sessions to examine the level of readiness of your group. Carefully outline the process necessary for getting the group ready for workcamping. Describe the expectations involved. Investigate any reservations about each person's ability to carry out assigned responsibilities.

Create support systems in your group for open discussions of workcamp possibilities. These same supportive relationships will help later if some of the group members fail to complete their tasks. Kids will feel better if they know they will be accepted even if they occasionally fall short of expectations, thus freeing them to correct the problems and move on.

Workcamps demand nearly a full year of effort. After a period of preparation and then doing the workcamp, more opportunities to serve may appear. Major choices will face a group after the workcamp. Re-entry into the local program creates a crucial time for planning and activity. Strengths gained at the workcamp will quiver in anticipation of being used. Unused, they will shrink and fade away.

Upon re-entry, the group should search for creative ways of involving the people who didn't attend the camp.

All workcamp participants should find ways to use their new-found abilities and experiences to draw others into your group. Focus your efforts on the growth of the group and the kingdom of God.

The group will be challenged to concentrate on personal service to others as the major concern for at least one year. Explore this challenge together to decide if your group can handle a workcamp. Your program of Christian growth will revolve around workcamping.

The effort will extend from the initial time of decision to the time when you make your reports and finish your spin-off projects. Many groups extend their service far beyond the actual workcamp as their excitement about being valuable servants propels them toward more efforts to serve.

Is Your Youth Group Ready?

Groups who thoughtlessly sign up for a fun trip to a new place will be handicapped by their misguided expectations. Young people must develop enough spiritual maturity to see the value of Christian service. Clearly defined purposes and goals will lead the group into such an understanding. This growth must begin long before leaving for a workcamp.

Your decision about workcamping will be made quickly if the group members want mostly personal enjoyment. They'll have a lot of difficulty understanding the self-giving love that drives Christians to help others. A workcamp is not merely a fun week away from home for self-centered kids. By clarifying a workcamp's purpose, you can avoid unpleasant surprises and smoldering resentment. Kids can decide before getting involved that workcamps don't excite their interest.

Stressing that mission and service are the focus of workcamps ensures that group members are not caught by surprise when the work begins. At the same time, though, workcamps are also a great deal of fun. When young people share a mission of love, they'll enjoy what they're doing.

If the group members can commit themselves to a workcamp with these understandings, they are mature enough to consider workcamping.

As you assess your group members' abilities to maintain their responsibilities throughout the year of preparation for a workcamp, consider these realities:

1. You'll invest tremendous effort in raising funds.

2. You'll test group members' self-discipline when they face a big cleanup job after a chili supper or other fund-raising event.

3. Kids will have to sacrifice some of their other activities in order to work at fund-raising projects and attend community-building group meetings.

4. Kids will be needed to plan every detail of the workcamp.

5. Numerous phone calls and letters will be needed throughout the year.

6. Double-checking will become a way of life that increases in importance as the project grows closer.

7. Traveling together will stress those who can't accept the quirks and needs of others in the group. Some kids will actively resist giving up personal pleasures for the benefit of the total group. Listening to music on a bus, for example, can throw a group into major arguments.

Adjustments are essential. A willingness to compromise will determine the outcome of conflicts in the group. Flexibility will be important as the group works out acceptable guidelines for traveling together.

8. Unexpected needs may suddenly hit the group when accidents occur, a vehicle breaks down or someone becomes ill. Even rainstorms during a tour of a zoo or an afternoon at the beach can demand quick personal adjustments to new situations.

9. Living together in a small space may make young people feel like captives as they sit in a vehicle for long hours. Again, a certain level of maturity will be essential.

10. Venturing into new territory may shock your group members. They will see new cultures and practices that are very different from their own experience. Poverty areas will present different value systems and lifestyles. Everything may look exotic. Judgmental attitudes and defensive rejection can tear a group apart. But personal control will save the group from major problems.

11. Kids will learn new skills while under pressure. They'll find ways to complete a project by the end of their scheduled work period. They'll grow in wisdom and experience.

12. Your group probably will endure primitive living conditions in a poverty area. Showers and restrooms will not be as nice as the ones back home. Or kids may even need extra creativity to improvise their own showers.

13. Maintaining health standards will add extra work. Those who become too lazy to brush their teeth when they are tired will receive some social pressure from the rest of the group. And simply washing your hands before eating will take on a new level of importance.

These stresses flourish during work trips. They can be endured, but they will pressure each person in the group. Your group will need to anticipate surprises and problems. Living and working together will test your group's determination to get along with one another. Maturity will help everyone.

14. Adult sponsors must understand their role as nurturing and affirming people. They will function best as support systems when the group deals with conflicts. Overbearing adults may diminish young people's self-esteem and self-confidence. But mature adults will serve as catalysts for growth. They'll stimulate thought and discussion. They'll encourage young people to resolve conflicts. They'll allow the group to grow at its own pace. The adults' maturity will reflect on everything that happens in the group. (But young people will take charge of the action.)

Your group's readiness for a workcamp depends on

these factors. Carefully assess your group's ability to handle these functions.

Is Your Church Ready?

The church will face the challenge to understand, accept and support the workcamp mission. Big dreams need a realistic foundation. If your church supports your efforts, you'll enjoy enlisting support. Fund raising will be more effective. Fewer complaints will arise. More resources and ideas will be offered as you plan in an environment of excitement and affirmation.

Consider the church's history of support for missions. Has any group carried out a work project? Is any church group actively serving the community with projects or activities? Does your church budget show generous support for missions at home and abroad? Do you hear a concern for missions preached from the pulpit? Are missions materials circulated in your church and actively used by the members?

These questions will form a basis for your assessment of the church's attitude toward a workcamp effort. Since a workcamp project may attract new people to your church, you also need to consider other vital questions:

1. How well does the church support its youth ministry?

2. Can we handle more people in our group and in our church?

3. Can we effectively accept and incorporate new people into our fellowship?

4. Are we ready to accept changes in our group?

5. Do we have the leadership (including adults and young people) within the group to accomplish this project and the growth it may foster?

If your assessments indicate that your young people, youth group and your church are ready, you can go on with the preparation. Use the information gained from the appraisals to plan instruction throughout the year. Increase kids' level of spiritual maturity by focusing several Bible studies on servanthood. Plan short service projects during the year to increase kids' endurance and work skills. Continually build feelings of closeness and community within the group that will support it throughout the workcamp experience.

Sample Time Line

Let's look at a sample time line for planning a summer workcamp with your youth group. Spreading out these events over several months ensures that the process will go smoothly, yielding maximum results for your group.

November

_____ Consult your pastor about the idea of taking the youth group to a workcamp.

_____ Gain approval from the proper board or commission in your church to investigate the possibilities of a summer workcamp experience for your group.

_____ Survey your congregation and youth group members to evaluate their readiness for a workcamp experience.

_____ Present a general idea of the workcamp to the youth group. Then, select a small team of interested kids and adults to serve as a steering committee and to help plan each step. Think of ideas to motivate the youth to participate in a workcamp.

_____ Choose a particular workcamp. Decide whether you want to plan a workcamp of your own, or go to an established one.

_____ Develop a preliminary budget and a fund-raising plan.

_____ Present a detailed proposal to the youth group.

_____ Develop strategies for gaining the backing of the parents and congregation.

_____ Meet with the parents and congregation. Give them a clear picture of the benefits of workcamping.

_____ Set up task forces of kids and adults to plan specifics in areas such as travel plans, menus, budget, fund raising, devotions, skills training, etc.

December

_____ Set a deadline for young people to commit to the workcamp. Require them to turn in a deposit on a specific date.

_____ Reserve space in a particular workcamp by sending an application form and deposits for the number of spaces you will need.

_____ Continue exploring meanings of Christian servanthood and discipleship with the youth group.

_____ Initiate fund raising.

January and February

_____ Determine transportation needs. Make needed reservations for vehicles and drivers. (Procedures vary from workcamp to workcamp; however, in most settings your vehicles will be needed to transport crews to work sites.)

_____ Continue fund-raising efforts.

_____ Determine travel routes to and from the workcamp. Arrange for lodging if needed. (Churches and colleges are good sources for lodging along the way, and using them helps keep your travel expenses low.)

_____ Determine fun activities for your group en route. Make necessary arrangements and reservations. (For example, canoeing, rafting, amusement parks, water parks, points of interest, etc.)

_____ Plan a pre-workcamp skills-training program for later in the spring.

March and April

_____ Do role plays to acquaint your group with the realities of poverty and with the dynamics of teamwork and communication.

_____ Have some young people and adults research the

culture of the area and report to the youth group.
_____ Continue fund-raising projects.

May

_____ Conduct the pre-camp training program.
_____ Continue special programming with the group
members to prepare them for the experience. Discuss their
expectations. (What do they expect to give? receive? How
do they feel they will be challenged? How does the Christian faith fit into this experience?)
_____ Meet with adult leaders who will attend the workcamp. Establish responsibilities, and talk over rules and
guidelines for your group. Discuss the young people's
expectations for the workcamp experience, and discuss
expectations you, as adults, have for the young people.
_____ Organize and assign responsibilities for your trip:
budget, food allowance, bus or van maintenance and
cleanup, packing and unpacking, map reading, communication between vehicles, first aid and emergency plans and
preparation.
_____ Plan a congregational "send-off" experience. This
could be a short element in a worship service or other
churchwide meeting.
_____ Send parents a list of what the young people need
for the trip.
_____ Continue fund-raising efforts.

June

_____ Double-check all reservations for your trip.
_____ Gather tools for the workcamp. Mark them in some
way so they can be claimed when your group returns. (For
example, color code all tools by wrapping colored tape
around the tool handles.)
_____ Brainstorm follow-up ideas to use with your kids
after the workcamp. (Capitalize on their experiences and
motivate them to continued growth.)
_____ Plan ways to report the workcamp experience to

the congregation after the camp. (You might plan a thank-you banquet for parents.)

_____ Plan ahead if you want slides and taped interviews of your workcamp experience. (One group brought three or four inexpensive cameras and several rolls of film. The young people took pictures each day of the workcamp. They had slides of every member of their group upon returning home. The group also brought several inexpensive tape recorders and interviewed residents and participants.)

_____ Go to the camp and experience servanthood.

_____ Return home and make plans for future projects in your area.

_____ Implement plans to include new people in your group.

Chapter Four

Visioning the Opportunities

O nce you've assessed the readiness of your young
people, youth group and church, you're ready to
match your group with an appropriate workcamp experience. This matching process requires careful consideration of a variety of factors. Your group may be better
suited for one type of workcamp than another. In this
chapter we will survey various kinds of workcamps that
emphasize certain aspects of workcamping.

Do not attempt this matching process alone; give
others a chance to help. Present the basic idea of a workcamp to the youth group, then ask for a few young people
and adults to serve as a steering committee to guide the
workcamp planning and the preparation.

Include a mixture of ages on the steering committee.
Give teenagers as well as adults the responsibility for developing rules and policies. Teenagers can view the overall
perspectives of the workcamp, then suggest policies and
guidelines for the approval of the rest of the steering committee. The steering committee as a whole will work to
maintain all church policies and enforce the group's rules.

A youth group in Colorado wanted to go to a GROUP
Workcamp in South Carolina. A steering committee was
formed to organize the preparations. Committee members
included two representatives from each grade in high
school, two adult sponsors and the youth pastor. The
steering committee prepared the groundwork for the experience, then invited other youth group members to

work on planning task forces for specific areas such as food, lodging, recreational side trips, and so on. (Chapter 7 gives more details on setting up task forces.)

Have your steering committee help you review the information gathered from the assessment forms in the previous chapter. Carefully examine all the information. The better the match, the more your group will grow at a workcamp.

Consider the ages of people in the group. Are there more older members or more younger members? Can the group members concentrate on an issue until it is resolved? Or do they change the subject before an issue is decided? Are the group members generally more or less mature for their age level?

Trust your feelings to guide this subjective evaluation. Your assessment of your group's maturity obviously is a value judgment. There will be no clear-cut, perfect answer. Your judgment will be based on information gathered from personal observation and intuition.

If your members are younger, they may need the influence of older, more stable young people or adults in their work crew. They may need simpler projects that require less time to complete. They may require less travel to get to a project location. A younger group will need more supervision and more skills training along with shorter work periods and less strenuous projects.

Beginners at a workcamp will grow more with less difficult demands. Select simpler projects and comparatively safe work environments. A local workcamp may be all a younger group can handle. If so, a local workcamp will prepare a younger group for more challenging experiences in subsequent years.

Older groups present other kinds of concerns. You may need to schedule around the members' summer jobs. Someone will need to talk with their supervisors to arrange for a period of absence during the summer months.

These groups will demand a more challenging work project. A simple job may bore them. Travel plans should offer interesting side trips. Consider interaction with other youth groups as a factor in maintaining their interest.

More experienced and articulate young people will also enjoy new and different cultures for their work environment. They will want a challenge for their level of spiritual maturity.

If your group includes a mixture of many different levels of maturity, look for an opportunity to use their various strengths. Veteran youth group members can help guide the growth of the newer members. They can also function as peer supervisors because of their experience and common sense.

Some groups pair the older and younger members into prayer partners. Each person is responsible for affirming and encouraging the other throughout the entire project period. A specific responsibility will bring out strengths and skills that were previously unused and untested.

As you evaluate the young people's needs, consider their unique characteristics as opportunities to optimize their growth. More experienced members can help beginners understand servant scriptures, explaining how these passages influence the group's decisions.

Your biggest consideration for matching your group to a particular form of workcamp will be your church's attitude. Do people in your church enjoy giving and serving? Do church people already express positive opinions about workcamps? Does the church strongly favor one type of workcamp over another? Is the workcamp location a major issue? Are there any leaders who can help you determine the mood of the church?

Some groups start small and grow toward more dramatic forms of workcamping. Others feel free and even obligated to launch out with the biggest challenge they can find.

Looking at Nationally Organized Workcamps

Denominational programs are available to many groups. Simply contact your national office to see what opportunities exist. Most of these programs cater to individual groups. Depending on the size of your group, you would go to a certain locality and work on an individual project. Evening programs often are left up to local leadership. Sometimes, though, groups can take advantage of prepared programs with cultural presentations and interaction with local residents.

Independent interdenominational programs offer many experiences in different parts of the country. These programs have special features that may interest some groups more than others.

Ask the steering committee to help you evaluate the workcamp opportunities by reviewing the list of organizations that sponsor workcamps (see the Appendix). Think about the pluses and minuses your group might experience with each kind. Call the organizations you are interested in and ask them these questions:

1. Who can attend?
2. Are there any restrictions (such as denominations)?
3. What's the age range of participants?
4. Are individual registrations accepted? group registrations? What is the required ratio of leaders to young people?
5. How long does the camp last?
6. How many people are usually involved in each camp?
7. What does it cost?
8. What does the cost cover? (Does the fee include insurance? If so, what are the coverages and exclusions? If not, how does the organization expect to handle medical and liability responsibilities?)
9. What are additional expenses, if any?
10. What are the policies regarding deposits, balances

due and refunds?

11. How is training carried out?

12. Is evangelism emphasized?

13. Are evening programs offered?

14. Are Bible studies or devotionals planned?

15. Who supervises the projects?

16. Does the work area change each year or stay the same?

17. How many workers will the program accommodate?

18. What range of dates does the program cover?
   ☐ June
   ☐ July
   ☐ August
   ☐ Other _____

19. What else should I know?

Planning Your Own Workcamp

Some churches decide to organize their own workcamp—locally or in another area. If you want to do this, look once again at your group and the resources available in your church. Are there enough adults available and willing to help put together the work project? Will the adult leadership have the time to select projects? to write out work descriptions? to estimate the materials needed? to select appropriate tools? to supervise the work? to ensure safety during the project?

Are there enough mature and experienced young people to form a solid foundation for the program? Will the young people commit to a program of hard work in their local community? Will they sacrifice time from jobs and reject spontaneous invitations to have fun with their friends? Will they ignore other summer programs to complete the project as planned? Will parents protect the time committed to the work project by scheduling family vacations and other functions around the work period? Will you, as the youth group coordinator, have time to organize a local workcamp?

If you can affirmatively answer these questions, you could handle your own project. Once you have decided to set up your own workcamp, then investigate your options for places to work. Check with your pastor or other outreach workers to discover people who need home repairs but can't do the work themselves or afford to pay for it.

Find other projects by visiting local agencies such as a community action program or weatherization office. These programs usually follow strict guidelines for making expenditures, so they usually welcome help from a group willing to tackle projects that fall outside established guidelines.

If you are considering setting up your own workcamp in another locality, you'll need a local contact person and agency with which to work. Choosing a local agency to help coordinate your efforts includes several criteria:

1. Does the agency have direct contact with people who are poor, elderly or in need of special help?

2. Are there enough workers in the agency to allow some of them to assist with arrangements for your workweek?

3. Does the agency have established guidelines for working with poverty-level clients?

4. Are funds available for materials that could be used by your workers?

5. Has the agency worked with other groups before?

6. Do you sense an understanding and acceptance of your project?

7. Is the agency convinced of your commitment to complete your projects?

8. Will agency leadership assist with coordinating the project?

9. Will adequate communication and planning be possible over a prolonged preparatory period?

10. Will the agency plan to obtain and deliver materials in preparation for your group's arrival, or will you need to make these plans yourself?

You will be able to offer the agency free labor. You

also can provide some funds for purchasing materials. Discuss with the agency the amount of money needed for materials. Try to plan your budget to include an adequate amount to finish all your projects. You also will need to provide tools. The local agency should supply large or cumbersome equipment such as ladders and wheelbarrows since such equipment is difficult to transport.

During the work project, agency personnel will need to conduct daily quality checks. Skillful supervision will prevent major problems. If a crew doesn't understand the work description or uses a technique that is unacceptable under the agency's guidelines, supervisors can instruct the crew.

Clear communication and adequate supervision help avoid frustrating mistakes. Groups of young people sometimes have had to tear down a day's work because they started in the wrong way. Some have applied wall siding vertically instead of horizontally and had to take it off and start again the next day.

Planning your own workcamp places other logistical demands on the group as well. Someone will need to prepare meals and provide snacks. Crews and tools must be transported to work sites. An adult working at the work site is essential, and adults should drive the vehicles.

You will be making a judgment call about your group's ability to plan and complete its own workcamp. Assembling information and evaluating it carefully will guide your opinion. While making your decision, consider these questions as guidelines for your final analysis: Is the group ready to work with one another and maintain a cooperative Christian spirit? Does the group get along well enough to face the stress of hard work, blisters, new surroundings and unforeseen problems? Is the group's leadership prepared to carry all the responsibilities involved in preparing, organizing, operating and completing a workcamp?

Consider the differences between traveling to a work area and doing the work in your home community. Each has its own advantages.

Advantages of traveling to a workcamp:

1. Your group will enjoy the adventure of traveling to new places.

2. Unless your church is in a severely depressed community, you usually can select an area with greater need than at home.

3. A new and different culture can excite your group.

4. You'll leave behind the interruptions caused by family and friends.

5. Your group will live together 24 hours a day working, eating, sleeping and traveling together.

6. You'll commit more time and money to the project.

7. A successful workcamp experience away from home fires up young people to prove what they can do at home. (Attending a distant workcamp first often encourages local service later.)

Advantages of staying at home for a workcamp:

1. You will be helping a neighbor in your local area.

2. The church will see firsthand the effects in the community.

3. Public relations for your church might carry more impact.

4. You can use more volunteer resources during the workweek.

5. A workcamp at home could cost less, or you could use more money for materials and less for travel.

6. Young people will feel their commitment in their normal living environment.

7. The young people as well as the church as a whole will be exposed to the real needs in their own community.

Comparing Workcamp Opportunities

Use Chart 4 to help you decide between a self-organized workcamp (at home or away) or a nationally planned one. Use a scale of 1-5 (1=low; 5=high) to rate the workcamp opportunities according to what they offer in these areas: project complexity; training available; project length; commitment of youth group; support of church; amount of interference with project (for example, willingness of kids to take off time from work, or willingness of parents to schedule vacation on other dates); evening activities offered; project cost; travel cost; and possibility of side trips.

Note that some nationally planned workcamps offer features that others don't. Consider how each workcamp might provide an opportunity to meet your group's goals. Also consider how each workcamp provides opportunities to improve on some of the group's weaknesses.

After you compare the opportunities, decide whether you want to organize your own workcamp or go to one that's already planned. If you decide to organize your own workcamp, begin the search for projects. If you decide to go to one that's already planned, rank your top three choices according to how well they match your group's needs and goals.

Ask the steering committee to present these choices to the youth group, then have the youth group vote on the camp they want to attend. Once you have informed the kids, set up task forces to plan details for each area of the workcamp preparation. Chapter 6 gives more information on presentations to the youth group, parents and congregation. Chapter 7 discusses task forces and their duties.

Matching your group with the best workcamp opportunity will challenge your best judgment. Jesus warns us to count the cost of any commitment we make (Luke 14:28-30). Careful plans, complete organization of every detail and wise choices will provide a life-changing experience for your group.

Chart 4
Comparative Rating of Workcamp Types

Rate the following factors for each type of workcamp by using a scale of 1-5 (1 = definitely NOT for our group; 5 = definitely IS for our group):

A. Self-Organized Workcamp: At Home
1. Appropriate project complexity: 1 2 3 4 5
2. Training available: 1 2 3 4 5
3. Good project length: 1 2 3 4 5
4. Commitment of youth group: 1 2 3 4 5
5. Support of church: 1 2 3 4 5
6. Evening activities, programs offered: 1 2 3 4 5
7. Project cost (food, activities, registration):   1 2 3 4 5
8. Travel cost: 1 2 3 4 5
9. Side trips possible: 1 2 3 4 5
10. Overall rating by steering committee: 1 2 3 4 5

B. Self-Organized Workcamp: Traveling
1. Appropriate project complexity: 1 2 3 4 5
2. Training available: 1 2 3 4 5
3. Good project length: 1 2 3 4 5
4. Commitment of youth group: 1 2 3 4 5
5. Support of church: 1 2 3 4 5
6. Evening activities, programs offered: 1 2 3 4 5
7. Project cost (food, activities, registration):   1 2 3 4 5
8. Travel cost: 1 2 3 4 5
9. Side trips possible: 1 2 3 4 5
10. Overall rating by steering committee: 1 2 3 4 5

C. Nationally Organized Workcamp _____
(Name of Organization)
1. Appropriate project complexity: 1 2 3 4 5
2. Training available: 1 2 3 4 5
3. Good project length: 1 2 3 4 5
4. Commitment of youth group: 1 2 3 4 5
5. Support of church: 1 2 3 4 5
6. Evening activities, programs offered: 1 2 3 4 5
7. Project cost (food, activities, registration):   1 2 3 4 5
8. Travel cost: 1 2 3 4 5
9. Side trips possible: 1 2 3 4 5
10. Overall rating by steering committee: 1 2 3 4 5

Mark your findings on the following diagram. Compare the various workcamps at a single glance.

	Appropriate Project Complexity	Training Available	Good Project Length	Commitment of Youth Group	Support of Church	Evening Activities, Programs Offered	Project Cost (food, activities, registration)	Travel Cost	Side Trips Possible	Overall Rating by Steering Committee
Self-Organized: At Home										
Self-Organized: Traveling										
Nationally Organized (List names)										

Permission to photocopy this chart granted for local church use only. Copyright © 1987 by Group Books, Inc., Box 481, Loveland, CO 80539.

Chapter Five

Budgets and Fund Raising

Workcamps will seem costly, especially after you add the costs of travel, materials, tools, program fees, etc. If these costs appear overwhelming, read again the first two chapters. The *benefits* of a carefully prepared workcamp experience far exceed the costs. I believe the investment in workcamping returns itself many times in the spiritual growth of youth and the people they help.

Budgets and fund raising are, therefore, important parts of a workcamp experience. Budgets list costs needed to complete the project successfully, and fund raising seeks to cover those costs. This chapter helps you prepare budgets (a preliminary one with estimated costs, and a final one with more definite costs) and gives you ideas for raising funds.

Preliminary Budget

Prepare a preliminary budget for church leaders. They will want to see a reasonably accurate estimate of the investment necessary for a workcamp. If you still haven't decided whether you want to plan your own workcamp or go to one that's already planned, you'll need budget figures for each option. If you *have* chosen one or the other, you'll only need to prepare one preliminary budget.

However, comparing the cost of each may make the decision for you. Some groups choose a local camp because they simply can't raise enough money to pay for both the workcamp and a long trip. Others choose an established workcamp so they won't have to worry about estimating the cost of food and supplies.

Your preliminary budget should include estimates of all essential items. The estimates should be as accurate as possible. More detailed costs can be worked out after the trip is approved. Survey several options as you estimate costs. For example, look at lodging possibilities such as camping out or staying at motels and colleges. You may want to adjust these options to fit your final budget.

Make a few phone calls to estimate figures now. Look for bargains later when you have more time and know the number of kids who have signed up. At this point, just prepare a reasonable plan and figure basic costs. Don't overestimate these costs, since a large budget will frighten some people in the church.

Organizing your own workcamp will require careful planning to cover all daily expenses such as meals, lodging, breaks, first aid, evening programs or activities and a contingency fund. (Chart 5 guides your budget planning for these items. Chart 6 helps you describe each work project and estimate costs.)

Travel costs will include renting or operating a vehicle or vehicles, along with gas and oil. If you prefer commercial charters or common carriers, telephone for information. Costs may be substantially more or less than you would guess. Rental costs can be estimated quickly with just a few phone calls to local agencies and national rental companies.

Figure out the travel distance to and from the workcamp location. Estimate your daily travel costs to and from the work project. Then add recreational side trips as options that make up a total package.

Carefully check vehicles' insurance coverage. Participants should have their own medical and accident insurance. Liability insurance will protect you in case of accidents at a work site or in a lodging facility.

Final Budget

Before preparing an exact budget and schedule, be sure you do three things:
- Gain approval from church leaders;
- Decide specifics on which workcamp you want to attend; and
- Have a definite number of kids signed up.

If you organize a local workcamp, planning for travel and lodging won't be necessary. However, if you want the group to stay together and enjoy some recreational side trips before or after the work project, you'll need a complete budget.

And if you organize a workcamp in another area, you will put together a more complex budget.

Daily expenses for a prepared national workcamp will be easy to figure. For example, GROUP Workcamps provide everything your group will need once you arrive. The registration fee covers all essentials, including insurance, work project materials, food and lodging, evening programs, and gas to get to and from the work sites. Of course, you will still need to calculate travel expenses to and from the workcamp.

Depending on your choice of workcamps, adapt Charts 5 and 6 for your final budget planning.

Your budget will be formed around the number of people who make a definite commitment to the workcamp. Ask each person to sign a statement of commitment and make a monetary deposit. Chart 7 is an example of a commitment statement.

By asking each person to invest his or her personal money for the deposit, you will know that you have a firm commitment from that person. Set the amount of the deposit so that it will impress each person with the importance of a definite decision.

You must secure dependable numbers for your planning to succeed. Project coordinators will not want

(text continued on page 78)

Chart 5
Workcamp Budget Worksheet

Location or Name of Workcamp _____
  I. Food Cost Estimates
    A. During Travel
      1. Per person estimated cost per day:
        a. breakfast: _____
        b. lunch: _____
        c. dinner: _____
        d. per person total cost per day: _____ (add lines a,b,c)
      2. Number of people: _____
      3. Total group cost per day: _____ (multiply line d × line 2)
      4. Number of days traveling: _____
    ★ 5. Total cost of food during travel: _____
        (multiply line 4 × line 3)
    B. During Workcamp
      1. Per person estimated cost per day:
        a. breakfast: _____
        b. lunch: _____
        c. dinner: _____
        d. per person total cost per day: _____
        (add lines a, b, c,)
      2. Number of people: _____
      3. Total group cost per day: _____ (multiply line d × line 2)
      4. Number of days at workcamp: _____
    ★ 5. Total cost of food during workcamp: _____
        (multiply line 4 × line 3)

  II. Lodging Cost Estimates
    A. During Trip
      1. Average cost per room: _____
      2. Number of people per room: _____
      3. Number of people in group: _____
      4. Number of rooms needed: _____ (divide line 3 by line 2, add 1 room for any remainder)
      5. Total group cost per day: _____ (multiply line 4 × line 1)
      6. Number of days during travel: _____
    ★ 7. Total cost for lodging during travel: _____
        (multiple line 6 × line 5)
    B. During Workcamp
      1. Average cost per room: _____
      2. Number of people per room: _____
      3. Number of people in group: _____
      4. Number of rooms needed: _____ (divide line 3 by line 2, add 1 room for any remainder)

5. Total group cost per day: _____ (multiply line 4 × line 1)
6. Number of days during workcamp: _____
★   7. Total cost for lodging during workcamp: _____ (multiply line 6 × line 5)

III. Transportation Cost Estimates
   A. During Travel
      1. Vehicle cost per day: _____
      2. Vehicle cost per mile: _____
      3. Estimated total miles: _____
      4. Miles per gallon (mpg): _____ (calculate for each vehicle if vehicles produce different mpg)
      5. Number of gallons needed: _____ (divide line 3 by line 4)
      6. Estimated cost per gallon: _____
      7. Total cost for gas: _____ (multiply line 6 × line 5; repeat calculations of lines 4 through 7 for each vehicle and add the amounts)
      8. Number of days of travel: _____
      9. Rental vehicle daily cost total: _____ (multiply line 1 × line 8)
      10. Rental vehicle mileage cost: _____ (multiply line 2 × line 3)
      11. Cost of transportation during travel: _____ (add lines 10, 9, 7)
      12. Cost of oil: _____ (approximately one quart per 1,000 miles, with oil changes at 3,000 mile intervals)
★   13. Total transportation cost during travel: _____ (add lines 11 and 12)

   B. During Workcamp
      1. Vehicle cost per day: _____
      2. Vehicle cost per mile: _____
      3. Estimated total miles: _____
      4. Miles per gallon (mpg): _____ (calculate for each vehicle if vehicles produce different mpg)
      5. Number of gallons needed: _____ (divide line 3 by line 4)
      6. Estimated cost per gallon: _____
      7. Total cost for gas: _____ (multiply line 6 × line 5; repeat calculations of lines 4 through 7 for each vehicle and add the amounts)
      8. Number of days of travel: _____
      9. Rental vehicle daily cost total: _____ (multiply line 1 × line 8)
      10. Rental vehicle mileage cost: _____ (multiply line 2 × line 3)
★   11. Total transportation cost during workcamp: _____ (add lines 10, 9, 7)

continued

Workcamp Budget Worksheet continued

IV. **Work Projects, Programs and Recreation**
   A. Materials for Work Projects
      1. Number of projects: _____
      2. Estimated average cost per project: _____
         (Use Chart 6. Total all project costs and divide by number
         of projects.)
      3. Total cost of materials for work projects: _____
         (multiply line 2 × line 1)
   B. Beverages for Breaks
      1. Total number of participants: _____
      2. Total number of days: _____
      3. Total cans of beverage needed: _____
         (multiply line 2 × line 1)
      4. Estimated cost per can: _____
      5. Total cost of beverages: _____ (multiply
         line 4 × line 3)
   C. Insurance
      1. Total number of participants: _____
      2. Cost per person per day for insurance: _____
      3. Cost per day for total group: _____ (multiply
         line 1 × line 2)
      4. Number of days to be insured: _____
      5. Total cost for insurance: _____ (multiply line
         4 × line 3)
   D. Evening Activities and Programs
      1. Number of activities and programs planned: _____
      2. Estimated cost per activity: _____
      3. Estimated cost per program: _____
      4. Average cost per activity and program: _____
         (add lines 2 and 3; divide by 2)
      5. Estimated total cost for activities and programs: _____
         (multiply line 4 × line 1)
   E. T-Shirts (Optional)
      1. Cost per shirt: _____
      2. Number of people: _____
      3. Total cost of T-shirts: _____ (multiply
         line 2 × line 1)
   ★ F. Total Work Projects, Programs, Recreation: _____
      (add A.3, B.5, C.5, D.5, E.3)
   SUBTOTAL: _____ (add the starred lines throughout
   the entire budget sheet)
   CONTINGENCY FUND: _____ (multiply the subtotal ×
   .2 for the recommended 20 percent)
   TOTAL BUDGET: _____ (add the subtotal and
   contingency fund)

Permission to photocopy this chart granted for local church use only. Copyright © 1987 by
Group Books, Inc., Box 481, Loveland, CO 80539.

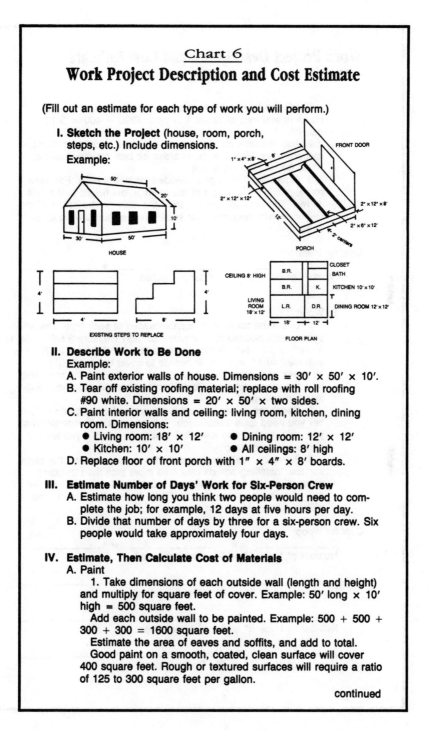

Chart 6
Work Project Description and Cost Estimate

(Fill out an estimate for each type of work you will perform.)

I. Sketch the Project (house, room, porch, steps, etc.) Include dimensions.

Example:

II. Describe Work to Be Done
Example:
  A. Paint exterior walls of house. Dimensions = 30′ × 50′ × 10′.
  B. Tear off existing roofing material; replace with roll roofing #90 white. Dimensions = 20′ × 50′ × two sides.
  C. Paint interior walls and ceiling: living room, kitchen, dining room. Dimensions:
   ● Living room: 18′ × 12′   ● Dining room: 12′ × 12′
   ● Kitchen: 10′ × 10′   ● All ceilings: 8′ high
  D. Replace floor of front porch with 1″ × 4″ × 8′ boards.

III. Estimate Number of Days' Work for Six-Person Crew
  A. Estimate how long you think two people would need to complete the job; for example, 12 days at five hours per day.
  B. Divide that number of days by three for a six-person crew. Six people would take approximately four days.

IV. Estimate, Then Calculate Cost of Materials
  A. Paint
    1. Take dimensions of each outside wall (length and height) and multiply for square feet of cover. Example: 50′ long × 10′ high = 500 square feet.
    Add each outside wall to be painted. Example: 500 + 500 + 300 + 300 = 1600 square feet.
    Estimate the area of eaves and soffits, and add to total.
    Good paint on a smooth, coated, clean surface will cover 400 square feet. Rough or textured surfaces will require a ratio of 125 to 300 square feet per gallon.

continued

Work Project Description and Cost Estimate
continued

Divide the total number of square feet by 400, or less for rough or textured surfaces. Example: 2200 ÷ 400 = 5 1/2 gallons.

2. Add amounts for trim around windows, doors and fascia, as necessary. Measure those areas for best results. Example: 6″ × 60′ = 30 square feet.

3. Figure amount of paint needed for inside walls. For each room, multiply the length of the room × the height of the ceiling × two. Then multiply the width of the room × the height of the ceiling × two. Add totals for square feet of inside walls to be painted.

Cost for Paint:

_____ × _____ = _____
Number of gallons   Cost per gallon

B. Wood

1. Count the number of boards needed of each type. The 4″-wide boards needed for the porch actually measure 3 5/8″. Use 12′ × 12″ to get 144″. Divide 144 by 3.625 (3 5/8) to get 39.72. You will need 40 1″ × 4″ × 8′ boards to cover the porch. (In all cases, measure the actual size of the material you are using to make your estimates. Careful measuring will make your estimates practical.)

2. Check the prices at local lumberyards for the grade of lumber you need for a specific job. Tell lumberyard personnel what you are repairing and ask what grade you need, if you are not sure what grade to buy.

3. Plywood usually costs more than boards to cover the same surface. Installing boards may take more time than installing plywood, but since you will have much free labor, saving time with plywood is not necessary. Cured boards that are painted will do a good job at less cost.

Cost for Wood:

_____ × _____ = _____
Number of 1″ × 4″ × 8′   Cost per board

_____ × _____ = _____
Number of 1″ × 6″ × 8′   Cost per board

_____ × _____ = _____
Number of 1″ × 8″ × 8′   Cost per board

_____ × _____ = _____
Number of 2″ × 4″ × 8′   Cost per board

_____ × _____ = _____
Number of 2″ × 6″ × 8′ Cost per board

_____ × _____ = _____
Number of 2″ × 8″ × 8′ Cost per board

_____ × _____ = _____
Number of 2″ × 10″ × 8′ Cost per board

_____ × _____ = _____
Number of 2″ × 12″ × 8′ Cost per board

Other wood

_____ × _____ = _____

_____ × _____ = _____

_____ × _____ = _____

Nails

_____ × _____ = _____
Number of pounds   Cost per pound

C. Roofing
1. Measure the area to be covered. Multiply dimensions to get square feet. Use coverage figures from packaging of the type of roofing you will use. Roll roofing that is lapped 4 to 6 inches costs less than shingles. Do not apply roofing over a third layer of old roofing material. Start with a bare roof.

Cost for Roofing:

_____ × _____ = _____
Number of rolls or   Cost per unit
squares

Nails for roofing

_____ × _____ = _____
Number of pounds   Cost per pound

Other materials

_____ × _____ = _____

_____ × _____ = _____

_____ × _____ = _____

_____ × _____ = _____

Permission to photocopy this chart granted for local church use only. Copyright © 1987 by Group Books, Inc., Box 481, Loveland, CO 80539.

Chart 7
Commitment Statement

I _____ will attend this summer's workcamp
     (Name)

from _____ to _____. I'll participate in
                  (Dates)

all fund-raising efforts and help with the planning. Along with this
commitment, I'll deposit _____ to confirm my inten-
                                  (Amount)

tions to participate.

I want to participate in the ministry of this workcamp because (add
reasons):

I can contribute these work skills, attitudes and personal abilities:

I agree to follow all rules and support the entire program with my
cooperation, enthusiasm and energies.

_____

Signature

_____

Date

Permission to photocopy this chart granted for local church use only. Copyright © 1987 by Group Books, Inc., Box 481, Loveland, CO 80539.

guesses about the number of workers to expect. A deposit that is not refundable will lead to a more stable registration number for the workcamp. Most people will think seriously before making a non-refundable deposit, so their decision will not fluctuate like it might with a verbal commitment.

Set a deadline for receiving the deposit and signed commitment. Encourage your total group to participate in the workcamp.

Group members who simply cannot afford the deposit should not be excluded from the workcamp experience for that reason. Ask generous church members to donate scholarships for these young people, and emphasize in your publicity and announcements that anyone who cannot afford to pay the deposit should see you. You may want to arrange for scholarship recipients to take on a special responsibility for the project to verify their commitment.

Set up a contingency list for group members who are uncertain about attending. Establish a deadline for this group to make a decision. You also could let them remain on a waiting list, in case someone else cancels.

One youth group began preparations for a workcamp after securing a verbal commitment from 15 kids. A deadline for registration and a deposit was never set. As the workcamp date grew closer, the number of interested kids dropped. By the time the workcamp arrived, only two kids wanted to go.

Firm numbers for planning will make preparation more complete. You also will build a more cohesive group if you set an early commitment time. The group members will form closer bonds as they work together toward their common goal. Following are items you need to consider when preparing your final budget:

1. Work project planning. Work descriptions require careful attention to many details. A workcamp organized by a national organization will prepare your projects for you. This type of workcamp lets you simply pay a registration fee and show up at the workcamp site.

However, if you are organizing your own work projects (either at home or at another area), follow these steps:

● *Estimate how many projects your group can complete in a week.* A typical day starts between 8 a.m. and 9 a.m., with departure from the site between 3 p.m. and 4 p.m. This time includes four to five hours of actual work per person for each day, and extra time for preparation, planning, breaks, lunch and cleanup. This average work period takes into consideration the lack of physical endurance the crew will have. Groups who try to put in more hours each day risk fatigue, which shows itself as poorer workmanship toward the end of the week.

If the group becomes too tired, safety also becomes more of a concern. A tired crew experiences more accidents. By returning from work at about 4 p.m., you also will have more time for the day's cooks to work. They'll want time to clean up a bit before beginning meal preparation before everyone starves.

A typical crew includes six people, evenly represented by males and females. Remember, inexperienced people will be doing much of the work. These crews will need more time than agency workers to complete the same amount of work.

Fill out one Work Project Description and Cost Estimate form for each work project (Chart 6) at least three months prior to the workcamp. Include materials needed, the quantity and cost of each item, and descriptions of the work to be done. Estimate how many days it would take a six-person crew to complete each project. If you can, work with local agency people to coordinate work projects. If you're on your own, ask a carpenter, contractor or handyman from your church to help you determine costs and time needed.

In the project description include the height of the building, pitch of the roof and steepness of the terrain around the house. That way you can double-check all safety factors for each project. A house built on the side of a steep hill or overlooking a river may endanger the crew. Ask about dogs or other animals on the property that could pose a threat to workers. You may need to take extra precautions to ensure safety in each of these cases.

● *Visit the work area and inspect the projects prior to the workcamp.* This visit will assure you that the group will have significant work to do. You'll also be able to identify projects that high school crews can't complete within the work period. The expense involved in this personal inspection may be prohibitive, however. If you can't afford a personal visit to the work area, communicate with agency workers by phone to clarify the description of the work.

Carefully determine whether every crew will have enough work for the whole week. The saddest problems happen when a crew is inspired to work but has nothing to do, because you're out of money or because the project lacks the proper materials, tools or directions. Careful planning and communication will prevent these problems.

During this visit, double-check the descriptions of the work projects to see if the materials lists match the jobs to be done. Compare your cost estimates with the agency's cost estimates. Be sure you both agree on the figures. Careful planning will save you many headaches later.

● *Plan your materials budget.* Ask the local agency workers if they will contribute some materials, and ask how much your group will be expected to pay. If your budget can't handle the projected amount of materials, negotiate for a project, such as painting, that uses less expensive materials. Sometimes a project description can be adjusted so more painting can be done, while more expensive parts of the project are dropped.

Plan to have a contingency fund to cover surprise expenses, breakage and mistakes that may be made by the work crews.

Sometimes an agency will be willing to negotiate a certain amount for materials expense. In this case, you would be responsible only for a specific amount of money. You still should maintain a contingency fund in case of problems. But the agency should not plan to use the contingency fund. If no surprises occur, you'll carry some money home with you.

A good procedure for arranging payment with a local agency is to pay in advance no more than 50 percent of the materials cost, with the remaining one-half due when materials are delivered to the work site. This arrangement gives you some leverage to ensure that there will be enough work for every crew. Payment for the remainder of the materials can be dependent on approval of the work site after your group has arrived. Your approval will be expected, if the project description and materials delivery have been handled effectively.

Some local contact people will not have enough money to purchase materials before your arrival. You may need to arrange for early arrival at the project location to visit the site and re-estimate the materials needed. Then you'll need time to purchase and deliver the materials before the project begins.

● *Communicate openly and continuously with the agency's contact person.* If you work with agency people, they will carry the main responsibility for preparing the work site. Develop good communication with key people so you'll always know the status of your work project.

Double-check the Work Project Description and Cost Estimate forms (Chart 6) and make final plans to acquire tools. You can make a special plea for loaners from your church, or you may need to rent special tools.

Ask the contact person to give you the exact mileage from your lodging to each work site. Also ask for a description of road conditions, along with an estimate of average speed on the way to the site. Double-check the amount of travel time necessary so you won't waste too much time that could be spent on work. Young people won't feel challenged by the work project if they spend two to three hours per day riding in a van.

Supervision of the work project will determine quality control. The local agency should provide experienced people who will check with the workers at least twice each day. Problems caught quickly are easier to fix than those that drag on for a day or two. Getting started the right way and having someone double-check the job will prevent frustration and costly mistakes.

Check with the contact person about ways to transport materials and workers to the work sites. You may need to revise your plans to get materials to the sites before work crews arrive. The first day will go more smoothly if all materials are on site and crews can concentrate on their work. Select places to store materials at each site so deliveries can be completed prior to the workweek.

Double-check the specific lodging arrangements for the number of people who will be working. Keep written records and receipts of all arrangements for lodging. List all reservation deposits paid in advance to hold your space. If you are staying in a camp, school or church, make a security deposit to assure your hosts that you will be careful with their property. You should also reassure them of your responsibility for any damages that occur.

Maintaining contact with agency people will help prevent unpleasant surprises at the last minute. Sustain periodic correspondence and make regular requests for reports on arrangements. As the time of the workcamp draws near, you'll need accurate and up-to-date information.

2. Schedule planning. Plan your schedule so you'll arrive early the day before the work begins. You'll need at least a full day to double-check your plans and complete your arrangements. You may need more time if the local coordinator is behind schedule. Group members can use the day to orient themselves to the new environment, to gather their tools, to rest and relax before working, and to receive training from local supervisors. Some crews can inspect their projects to prepare their minds for the next day. If problems with the work projects arise before you begin your trip, you may need to send someone to the work area several days ahead of the workcamp to correct the problems.

Allow money in your budget to cover expenses for evening programs and daily devotions. Ask the contact person for names of local people who could help with evening programs.

Young people will enjoy learning about local culture. The more active the presentations, the better. Ask local people to lead a sing-along session with banjos or lead the total group in cultural dances of the area. Special activities also will tickle the interest of the group. Make arrangements to visit cultural sites in the area. Let your steering committee choose and organize the best programs for evening sessions. See the Appendix for program and devotion ideas.

Young people will enjoy discussing the experiences of the day and putting them in Christian perspective. In the evening program, use the scripture passages from the daily devotions to clarify the meaning of their efforts. Then look ahead to the next day and the possibilities for discovering how God works in the workcamp. Clarify expectations for the next day's efforts by letting each person share.

Instruct leaders in each crew to stop work at appropriate times during the day. They can call attention to significant needs, insights or opportunities for going the second mile as a Christian. These opportunities may result from conflicts or problems. The leaders also should allow time to give thanks for friendship and for the beautiful work that is being done. Kids may describe the unusual actions of a resident or a time when God's presence was felt in a special way.

3. Food planning. This process will be based on the number of participants and the number of days scheduled for the trip. Budget a certain amount of money for food each day. Then, if eating in restaurants, specify a maximum that can be spent for each meal by each person. Explain to the participants that it will help the budget if they order within the limit, without trying to spend all the money available, whether they need that much food or not.

If you need to save money, cook your own meals. This approach works well if you have several young people who want to cook or who have experience with campground cooking. Plan to haul more equipment with you if you use the "economy-cooking" approach.

Menus will be necessary for each meal. Cooks must be trained and scheduled. Allow extra time for purchasing the food. The cooks will appreciate the time available to prepare the meals.

Schedule activities for those who are not cooking while the meal is prepared. Chores such as cleaning the bus or vans, setting up tents or setting the table will help keep everyone busy. If several people are scheduled to prepare the meal, divide the responsibilities so each person will have a comparatively small job.

Try to plan fun meals that include special desserts. You can have a dessert-making contest to see who can make the best pudding or the most colorful fruit cocktail.

Conduct surveys to discover if anyone has allergies or doesn't like certain foods. Plan your menu in advance and make copies so the group can make suggestions. Avoid excessive complaints by letting everyone comment on the menu.

If your workcamp involves travel, ask everyone to bring a sack lunch for the first day. Eating a sack lunch at a roadside park instead of eating at a fast-food establishment saves both time and money.

During the workweek, plan an ample breakfast, refreshments for a mid-morning break, a sack lunch and a scrumptious dinner. The sack lunch must contain items that won't spoil in case refrigeration isn't available. See Chart 8 for menu ideas. If you can, provide picnic coolers and ice for each crew to keep everything fresh. Bring plenty of cool water in addition to other beverages. Many water supplies at work sites are not safe for drinking—and hard workers need ample supplies of water.

Plan a shorter workday during midweek to give everyone a chance to regroup and recover some strength. Your group members will enjoy a relaxing change of pace by going to a nearby attraction or swimming pool. They'll regain some strength and develop a fresh attitude for the final days of work.

If you plan special meals or activities, include them in your budget. If you feel the individuals will have plenty of spending money, you can decide as a group whether or not the extra expense for the planned activity should be

---

Chart 8
Menu Ideas

Breakfasts
Fruit juice, milk or coffee
Cold cereal, bread or toast, and butter and jelly
Pancakes and bacon
Scrambled eggs and sausage
Omelets and hot cereal
Stuffed pancakes and ham
French toast and meat
Meat, and biscuits and gravy

Sack Lunches
Sandwiches filled with meat. Include packets of mayonnaise, mustard
    and catsup; pickles and lettuce in separate moisture-proof packets
Peanut butter and jelly sandwiches
Fruit, carrot sticks or celery
Potato chips or corn chips
Cookies or candy
Non-carbonated beverage

Dinners
Beverages
Tossed salad
Vegetables such as potatoes (mashed, baked or scalloped), corn,
    green beans, navy beans or lima beans
Bread, butter and jelly (dinner rolls or corn bread)
Entree such as roast beef, lasagna, spaghetti and meatballs or meat
    sauce, ham, pizza, hamburger, hot dogs, chicken or fish
Dessert such as cake, pudding, ice cream, pie or cobbler

   After everyone has eaten first servings, allow kids to take seconds.
Also, allow unlimited beverages.

---

budgeted or be an extra expense. Most groups like to include their activities in the total budget. If you release the group for free time at an amusement park, the individuals should pay for their own meals and rides.

4. Lodging. Lodging for the group while traveling will depend on the length of your trip. To save money, take tents for camping at campgrounds with showers. Moreover, group members can carry important responsibilities for cooking, and setting up and taking down the equipment. Since many young people have not experienced camping, they will see it as an adventure.

If you plan to camp out during the workweek, you'll need a secure campsite where your equipment will be safe while everyone is working. Always take valuables and money with you. Anything left behind could disappear. The same principle applies if you stay in a motel. However, some motels will lock your valuables in a safe.

A variety of facilities provide lodging. Check with college campuses, church-related schools, large churches with gyms or YMCA/YWCA organizations.

When you use a school for lodging, divide a large group into smaller groups with adults in each sleeping room. Then, if anyone coughs all night, only a few people are disturbed, rather than the whole group. (If all the adults snore, you have a big problem.)

Camping facilities usually fill up during the summer. But you may find enough space available for your group, so inquire about the possibilities for any campgrounds you can find.

Many churches will allow you to use their facilities. Often, you'll not find showers in churches, so you'll need to make other arrangements. If you can find adequate drains, temporary showers can be constructed. You'll need plastic curtains and portable shower heads using quick-attach hoses or adapters with threads to fit a garden hose. Secure permission (written, if possible) before improvising church facilities. See Chart 9 for more details on building a temporary shower.

5. Transportation and insurance. Vehicle expenses can be figured on a cost-per-mile basis. If you know the average miles per gallon of your vehicles, you can figure your estimated miles, divide by the miles per gallon, and then multiply that result by the estimated cost of gas for the area in which you'll be traveling.

Be sure to plan for oil changes during the trip if you'll be driving 3,000 miles or more. If you are pulling a trailer, you'll need to change the oil more often. Extremely hot or dusty conditions also require more frequent oil and oil

Chart 9
Shower Plans

Showers will freshen your group members and the air around them; however, some campgrounds and other public facilities don't provide showers. If that happens, you can make your own. These primitive arrangements will require workcampers to wear old bathing suits for a public washing.

Construct simple showers by using a rubber garden hose, hand-sprinkler attachment, faucet, electrical tape, boards, drill, hammer and nails. This makeshift arrangement works best if you have access to a sink with a single-outlet faucet. Then you can regulate the hot and cold water to achieve the right temperature for showers.

Cut off the metal end of the hose and slip the hose over the faucet. Tape it securely or use a ring clamp to tighten it to the neck of the faucet.

Run the hose to a nearby parking lot with adequate drainage. You could also use a room with a floor drain, if you can find one. Fashion an upright stand for the hose nozzle by drilling a 1-inch hole about 6 inches from one end of a 2″ x 4″ x 7′ board. Build a stand for it like the ones used for Christmas trees. Complete your shower facility by running the hose through the hole and attaching the sprinkler.

Check the size of the hot-water tank and estimate the length of time each person can shower to maintain hot water for everyone. (If you don't have hot water, the time will take care of itself.) You can shower in shifts, giving the tank enough time to recover its hot water. Directions on the tank may tell you the recovery time necessary.

Most groups prefer the opportunity to shower in regular showers. Possibilities include health clubs, swimming pools, campgrounds, churches, colleges and schools. You may spend a little more money, but the group will be happier.

filter changes, along with inspection of air filters and gas filters. Figure all possible expenses.

Emergency repair funds may bail you out of trouble. You'll need quick repairs and extra money if a tire blows out, the air conditioning quits in the middle of a desert or the water pump breaks. If you're using church-owned vehicles, the church may supply some emergency money in case of vehicle trouble. In any case, credit cards or travelers checks will furnish some peace of mind when something breaks.

Be sure you secure complete insurance coverage for the trip and work project. Your church's insurance agent can help you find extra coverage for the work you will be doing. Liability insurance, along with medical and accident insurance, will protect your group and your program. Include premiums for necessary insurance in the budget.

If the workcampers already have medical and accident coverage, ask them to bring proof of coverage on the trip. Then you may not need special medical and accident insurance.

Several insurance companies carry special camper and tourist policies. You can purchase this type of insurance on a daily or weekly basis. If you plan to go outside the United States, you'll need special insurance for vehicles, liability, medical and accident coverage.

Plan early deadlines for making arrangements for vehicles, lodging and work projects. Reservations made months in advance can save money. You'll also be more likely to reserve your first choice, rather than having to take second or third choices because you're too late.

6. Equipment. Equipment needs will grow out of your plans for food, projects and lodging. Budgeting for this expense will depend on the amount of equipment you'll be able to borrow from participants' families or other contributors.

Prepare a list of equipment needed: tools, cooking utensils, camping supplies. Let participants read the list to see if they will lend or donate any equipment for the workcamp. Your budget needs will grow significantly if you must purchase expensive tools or camping and cooking gear.

Hauling equipment may force you to rent a trailer or luggage racks for your vehicles. Some groups plan for a pickup truck to haul equipment. Then they use it during the workweek to haul materials to the work sites.

Expenses grow quickly if you must buy a lot of equipment and then rent a trailer to haul it. If the costs would be about the same for either arrangement, choose the way that best meets your goals for the trip.

7. Contingency fund. Plan at least 20 percent of

your total budget to cover all possible circumstances. If you would need to send someone home for disciplinary reasons, how would the fares be paid? If someone gets sick and the emergency room demands cash payment, will you have enough money to assure treatment?

A contingency fund gives you the flexibility to cover any expenses not planned in the budget. This fund should never be used to cover for sloppy budget planning. Use it only in the event of unforeseen costs. Have enough money in your contingency fund to cover unexpected needs in work projects, car maintenance and medical or personal emergencies.

Contingency funds can be used for future programs if they are not used during your project. You can enjoy a head start on your budget for the coming year or for another project. You also can carry over contingency funds from year to year as budget backups. More money will be earned through interest-bearing savings accounts until you are ready to travel again.

Interest-bearing accounts will also help as you begin raising money. Check various ways to deposit your funds so they can earn the highest interest rate and still be available when you need to make payments.

Fund Raising

Plan your fund-raising activities to exceed your total budget. Organize fund raisers such as workdays around the church. Have kids experience servanthood as they clean and repair church property.

One group of young people sold stock in their work-camp trip. They designed workcamp stock certificates and sold them for a dollar each. Congregation members invested in the workcamp program by buying the certificates. When workcampers returned after their experience, they thanked the benefactors by sponsoring a "stockholders" picnic.

Use the previously mentioned ideas and think of your own fund raisers. See the Appendix for other ideas.

Use Chart 10 to estimate how much money you'll need from each fund raiser. Estimate maximum and minimum income for each project. If your projects consistently make less money than you expected, you'll need to work

---

Chart 10
Fund-Raising Worksheet

Use this worksheet to estimate the amount of income needed from each of your fund-raising projects.

1. _____ Deposit to be paid by each participant

2. _____ Number of members attending

3. _____ Total amount of deposits from participants (multiply line 1 × line 2)

4. _____ Amount expected from church or youth ministry budget

5. _____ Total of lines 3 and 4

6. _____ Total amount needed for workcamp and trip

_____ Total needed from fund raisers (subtract line 5 from line 6)

Estimate the number of fund-raising projects you think your group can complete. Use Chart 11 to list the projects for each month. Divide the total amount needed from fund raisers by the total number of projects. This figure represents the average amount you will need from each project in order to meet your budget.

a. _____ Total amount needed from fund raisers

b. _____ Number of projects

_____ Average amount needed from each project (divide line a. by line b.)

If you think the average amount is too much or too little, adjust the number of projects to achieve the amount you think your group can handle to meet your proposed budget.

Permission to photocopy this chart granted for local church use only. Copyright © 1987 by Group Books, Inc., Box 481, Loveland, CO 80539.

harder to promote the fund raisers. Setting up more projects than you think you need will help make up the difference between your expectations and your results. Plan the extra projects as options to be used only if necessary.

Set a required number of hours for each participant to assist in the fund-raising projects. Establish guidelines for

---

Chart 11
Fund-Raising Projections

	Project and Date	Projected Income
September:	_____	_____
October:	_____	_____
November:	_____	_____
December:	_____	_____
January:	_____	_____
February:	_____	_____
March:	_____	_____
April:	_____	_____
May:	_____	_____
June:	_____	_____
July:	_____	_____
August:	_____	_____

Total fund-raising projected income: _____

Deposit amount × number of members:
_____ × _____ = _____

Total income from projects and deposits
(add the two totals from above):
_____

Permission to photocopy this chart granted for local church use only. Copyright © 1987 by Group Books, Inc., Box 481, Loveland, CO 80539.

making up hours if someone gets sick or has a schedule conflict. Firmly communicate to group members and adult volunteers that their participation will determine the success of the projects. Caution them not to use makeup hours, if they have any choice. The group will depend on everyone's help to complete the projects.

Set intermediate goals for numbers of hours for each person to work, so no one gets too far behind in meeting his or her obligation. Also plan monetary goals. Make a weekly comparison of the actual income with the planned income.

Make or buy a large calendar to cover the entire workcamp project. List your fund-raising projects and their dates. Schedule the participants to work on the various projects after checking with each person to resolve any scheduling conflicts. List the number of hours each person will be working on each project. Use Chart 11 to track fund-raising dates and income.

Designate coordinators for each project or major part of a project. They will be responsible for all plans and preparations. Meet with the coordinators to go over the details and deadlines for each part of the process. Schedule a meeting time for all fund-raiser coordinators to organize responsibilities.

Plan regular sessions with each participant to discuss his or her involvement and feelings about the work. These sessions will help you monitor the group's "pulse" on a regular basis.

Chapter Six

Presenting the Plans

A successful workcamp experience requires the full support of parents, church leaders and the congregation. Presenting your plans to these key people will help you assess their support for a mission project.

Meet with the steering committee and fine-tune some specifics. Whether you're planning your own workcamp or going to one that's already planned, you need to schedule a date for the project. If some of the young people have jobs, have them see if they can take time off. If vacation time for adults is an issue, ask them to clear possible dates. List your options for workcamp dates. Then set the date and plan your workcamp to fit the most needs of your group. Be sure that key people can attend during the date you've chosen.

You are ready now to write a proposal with the youth group steering committee. First, define a purpose or mission statement for the workcamp. Clarify the purpose and value of workcamping by reviewing servanthood scriptures such as Matthew 22:37-40 and Luke 10:29-37. See the Appendix for more examples of servanthood scriptures.

Explain the expected outcomes of the workcamp experience, keeping in mind these biblical understandings. A purpose statement sample: "Our goal is to be active servants of God by spreading his love and helping people in need. To help us experience our goal, we propose that our youth group participate in the Appalachian Mission Effort."

Include the following items in a presentation:

● The type of workcamp that best meets your needs.

● A travel itinerary.

● A list of needed equipment.

● Expected outcomes when the group returns and begins its program for the following year.

● Your budget and a large calendar that shows fund-raising projects, deadlines and anticipated income. Think of other contingency ideas in case some of the fund raisers don't raise the anticipated amount.

● Disciplinary actions and expectations for the preparation time and the workcamp.

● Charts, handouts and fact sheets to help people better understand the workcamp mission.

Present your ideas to the senior pastor and other church leaders. Ask for a recommendation of ways to approach the church membership with your proposal. Some churches will approve a workcamp quickly. Others will need a great deal of explanation and persuasion before granting approval.

Use the recommendations from the senior pastor and other leaders to outline a plan that fits the general church program and expectations.

Once you prepare all the information, the steering committee presents the plan to the youth group members for their ideas and opinions. Recruit youth group members to help with the presentations. Tell the kids that their help is needed to present the plan to parents and the congregation to find out how much members would support a workcamp experience. Parents, church leaders and congregation members will more likely back a program that shows the interest, enthusiasm and involvement of many of the kids.

Divide the kids into pairs and assign them different aspects of the workcamp to present. For example, have one pair describe a workcamp, another pair discuss the budget, and another present fund-raising ideas. Ask each team to write what it will say. Carefully rehearse each pair's presentation and list some questions or reservations that may arise. Coach the speakers to answer the questions with grace and knowledge.

For example, if you plan to travel to another area, someone may ask: "Why is it necessary to go outside the local community for a workcamp? Don't we have plenty of needs in our own town?" Remember, the church throughout its existence has sent representatives to areas where there were great needs. This mandate from God grows out of the power of his love. Christians should realize that we may be required to go the second mile in order to witness God's outreaching love.

Other benefits of going to another area for a workcamp include travel, understanding other cultures and working with young people from other churches.

Point out that workcamping will engage the church's teenagers (as well as adults) in a process of planting seeds of faith. These seeds will grow in the lives of young people, church leaders, interested observers and anyone who will be helped by the work projects. Jesus described the importance of planting seeds in his example of a tiny mustard seed that grows into a strong tree (Matthew 13:31-32).

The church will grow more visible as a servant community. People will see the activity generated by the workcamp. The youth group will be working to raise necessary funds, to plan the project and to report back to the church (often with ideas for projects in the local community). Residents will not forget the group's assistance. The young people themselves will be affected in a very special way. They'll feel God's presence during their mission.

Jesus clearly promised that he would be with his servants wherever they work. He also declared that his servants should be willing to go wherever he calls them. When servants are faithful in this way, God will honor them (John 12:26). See the first two chapters for more benefits of the workcamp experience.

Your presentations will require specific information.

Prepare a detailed list of items you want the presentation teams to cover. Church leaders and parents will want facts and a full outline of your plans. Careful preparation will reassure them that you can effectively carry out a major project. You also may create a feeling of support for servant ministry that will impact the church as well as the youth group.

When the teams make presentations to various groups, encourage openness in discussing all aspects of the workcamp. Listen carefully to the groups' concerns so you can research possible solutions. List specific questions that need to be answered. With this information, you can develop plans that will assure the project's effectiveness.

Use the Presentation Checklist (Chart 12) with each group to record the questions raised and information needed for future reports to that group. Identify areas of positive support from each group. For example, a handyman or carpenter could help train the young people; someone who loves to cook could help with fund-raising projects such as bake sales, or he or she could help with training for meal preparation.

Pray with your group before making presentations to the church. Your openness to God's presence during the preparation of your presentations will let you know that the project truly is according to his will.

Presenting Your Plan to Parents

Prepare carefully for your meeting with youth group parents. Start with a slide-and-sound show or a video presentation of a workcamp program. Dramatic pictures of a workcamp will excite the group and present general information.

GROUP Workcamps use both slide-and-sound presentations and videotapes for promotion. Slides project a bigger picture for large groups to see, unless a large video screen is available. These audio-visual aids generate enthusiasm for workcamping. They describe what happens and then present the responses of workers and residents

Chart 12
Presentation Checklist

This checklist covers details to prepare for a presentation, as well as questions to answer during a presentation. Take the checklist with you to the presentation and fill out the items as they come up during the presentation. Two people will work best, so one can present while the other fills out the checklist with responses from the group.

Name of group or organization (for example, parents, church board, mission board, etc.):

Presenters:

Date and time of presentation:

_____ Handouts prepared for everyone.
_____ Presenters have learned or memorized written explanations.
_____ Time allotted for presentation:
_____ This group generally supports the estimated cost of the work-camp. Explain.

_____ This group generally does *not* support the estimated cost of the workcamp. Explain.

_____ This group supports the proposed fund-raising program. Explain.

_____ This group does *not* support the proposed fund-raising pro-gram. Explain.

Concerns or suggestions raised by this group:

a.

b.

c.

The set time for a return visit and further explanation:

Permission to photocopy this chart granted for local church use only. Copyright © 1987 by Group Books, Inc., Box 481, Loveland, CO 80539.

who have participated in the program.

After this introduction, have the presentation teams tell about different aspects of the workcamp experience. Also ask several young people to tell why they want to go to a workcamp and why they believe a workcamp would be an important investment of love, energy, time and money.

Present a large calendar showing the fund-raising plans for each month and the step-by-step deadlines that will accomplish your goals. Explain contingency plans that would be put into effect if some of the fund raisers don't match your expectations.

Point out each person's responsibilities and the amount of the deposit. Explain that each teenager must spend a certain number of hours on fund-raising projects. Make it clear that everyone who attends the workcamp must meet these established minimums.

Point out that much of the fund raising will operate in the general community to draw funds from outside the church. This plan will relieve some of the financial pressure that a workcamp could create within the church family. Explain that you will want and need some financial support from the congregation. In return, you would expect to create a feeling of mutual mission as the project develops.

In particular, reassure parents that you anticipate total church support, not just parental support, for the program to work.

Describe matters of discipline during the preparatory period and during the workcamp. Describe any rules that will be imposed by the workcamp organization or agency with whom you will be working. Emphasize to parents that full cooperation will be expected of each person throughout the workcamp and during the preparation period. If you will be attending a workcamp located outside the local community, let the parents know that any major behavior problems will demand immediate action. Breaking major rules will necessitate sending the person home at the parents' expense. This action will be taken as a last resort, after everything else fails.

Parents also will need to understand that a medical/liability release form will be required for participation in a workcamp. Chart 13 is an example of a medical/liability release form. The form allows treatment to be performed in the event of an emergency or the need for medical assistance while away from home. A liability release simply assures agency personnel that they will not be held liable for accidents unless actual negligence can be proved.

Discuss the reality that some problems will arise in conjunction with a workcamp. Surprises are unavoidable, but every possible attempt will be made to avoid problems. Explain that the contingency fund is a resource to use if major problems occur.

Reassure parents that they will be kept informed about plans as they develop or change during the preparation for the workcamp. During the workcamp, a designated person will regularly report home on the progress and on other information of the total group. Individuals also will be able to contact home on occasion.

Write down the parents' questions or comments. Address these matters in your future planning.

Give the parents a schedule for necessary arrangements including the time when deposits and medical/liability release forms are due. Set a date for a final parents meeting when you will give them details about the arrangements for the workcamp, along with addresses and phone numbers if you will be traveling.

Offer a list of servant scriptures for those who are interested. Studying these scriptures will help parents catch some of the spiritual significance of the workcamp.

Ask for the parents' support with their prayers throughout the preparation period. Ask them to pray specifically that each person will grow through the workcamp experience according to God's will.

Close the meeting with a prayer. Ask the parents and presenters to express their hopes, their expectations and their need for God's guidance and love. Ask for a special blessing on your preparations so the workcamp truly will be an outpouring of God's love.

Chart 13
Release of All Claims

In consideration for being accepted by _____
Name of church

for participation in the workcamp at _____
Place

on _____, I (we) being 21 years of age or older,
Date

do for myself (ourselves) (and for and on behalf of my child-participant if said child is not 21 years of age or older) do hereby release, forever discharge and agree to forever hold harmless (Name of church), the directors, officers, employees and agents thereof, from any and all liability, claims and demands for personal injury, sickness and death, as well as property damage and expenses, of any nature whatsoever which may be incurred by the undersigned and the child-participant that occur while said child is participating in the above-described workcamp, which shall include travel between the child's home and the camp, excursions from the camp and time spent at the camp.

Furthermore, I (we) (and on behalf of our child-participant if under the age of 21 years) hereby assume all risk of said personal injury, sickness, death, damage and expense as a result of participation as above set forth.

Further, authorization and permission is hereby given to said organization to furnish any necessary transportation, food and lodging and to assign work to this participant.

The undersigned further hereby agree to hold harmless and indemnify said church, its directors, officers, employees and agents, for any liability sustained by said church as the result of the negligent, willful or intentional acts of said participant, including expenses incurred attendant thereto.

(If participant has not attained 21 years):

I (we) am the parent(s) or legal guardian(s) of this participant, and hereby grant my (our) permission for him (her) to participate fully in said workcamp, and hereby give my (our) permission to take said participant to a doctor or hospital and hereby authorize medical treatment, including but not in limitation emergency surgery or medical treatment, and assume the responsibility of all medical bills, if any, in excess of any applicable medical insurance coverage provided through this workcamp program. Further, should it be necessary for the participant to return home due to disciplinary action, for medical reasons or otherwise, I (we) hereby assume all transportation costs.

Type or print name of participant

Only participant need sign if 21 years of age or older. If under 21, *both* parents must sign unless parents are separated or divorced in which case the custodial parent must sign.)

Father	Date

or Custodial Parent	Date

Mother	Date

Participant	Date

Parent(s) telephone

Camp Participant Only

I have read the foregoing and understand the rules of conduct for participants and will abide by them as well as the directions of the leadership of the workcamp.

Participant	Date

Permission to photocopy this chart granted for local church use only. Copyright © 1987 by Group Books, Inc., Box 481, Loveland, CO 80539.

Presenting the Plan to the Congregation

The church's support is crucial to the success of a workcamp. Nurturing the support for your mission will help your fund raising and your asking church members to provide resources during the planning stage.

You'll want as many people as possible to know about the workcamp and support your efforts. To spread the word, prepare a general explanation for the church newsletter. Announce that the youth group presentation teams will visit each organization in the church to explain the workcamp program in more detail. Also say that you will make a presentation to the total congregation on a certain date—at a fellowship dinner, special meeting or regular worship service. Be sure your pastor or church leadership gives approval for this approach before you submit an announcement for the newsletter. Try to arrange to present your plans to smaller groupings to allow more opportunity for questions and answers.

When you present workcamping to church groups, clearly state your intentions. You are sharing information and asking for comments and questions to help with planning. You want everyone to understand the potential value and purpose of the project.

The presentations should be as brief as possible, but cover all major considerations. Explain the purpose or mission statement, budget and fund-raising plans, and give a description of the work project.

List any church members' questions or concerns that will be helpful in the decision-making process. Gather more information for subsequent presentations on the basis of the questions asked and concerns raised.

Give people in each group fact sheets to help clarify questions about the workcamp. (You also can get approval to insert fact sheets in the church worship bulletin or newsletter.) You can request voluntary contributions after the facts are presented; simply tell people how to make their contributions. (Be sure this approach is approved by the church leadership.) Many people will want to make special or personal gifts in addition to their other giving.

A slide-and-sound show or videotape will help you present the excitement of a workcamp. Be sure that whatever show you use presents an uplifting picture of the benefits of workcamping along with information about the work project. Each time you make a presentation in the church, you either will be helping or hurting the support you hope to receive from the church.

Ask the presentation teams to describe the various aspects of the workcamp. Always communicate the importance of mission. Explain the impact you expect the project to have in the local community. Point out the possibility of mission efforts after the workcamp. Remind listeners of the deeper concern for service that can be fostered through the workcamp.

Ask several leaders from the congregation to comment about their support for the project. Statements by known leadership lend validity to the workcamp in the eyes of the church. The senior pastor's affirmation of the spiritual benefits of a workcamp also are influential.

Describe the high points from your calendar of activities and any upcoming fund-raising projects you will sponsor. Provide opportunities for immediate response after the general presentation. Interest will be high in some people. Ask everyone to support and strengthen the mission through prayer.

Cultivating this support takes a great deal of time and energy. You will need to answer many questions and even respond to objections. But your efforts to inform the parents and church will pay off many times over through their support in prayer and personal resources. Don't take shortcuts through this process, or your workcamp might also be short-circuited.

Regular Progress Reports

Once every two months or so prepare an updated

report for the congregation and church leaders. Send youth presenters to various groups to report your current status and remind the church members of activities planned for the coming few weeks.

Create more enjoyment and understanding of your reports by sharing particulars about the workcamp. Present some aspect of the culture of the area you will visit. Describe something about the work project. Dress the presenters as painters one time, roofers another time. Have them dress in costumes representing the region where the workcamp will be held, or show posters depicting something about the area.

Progress reports can be fun, generating interest and enthusiasm. View them as opportunities, not duties. Present informational reports in the church newsletter or through worship bulletin inserts. Once a month, make brief announcements in the regular worship services.

Creative displays keep the workcamp in the minds of the congregation. Use large posters to display pictures of the youth group participating in a fund-raising project. Create a picture album showing lots of people from the church attending the fund raisers and service projects. Show up-to-date progress in your fund-raising program. Some groups have used the thermometer graphic to show the current level of funds moving toward the completed budget amount at the top.

One effective display that often is used as a fund raiser is a drawing of a huge road map going to and from the workcamp. The map can be divided into mile segments that are highlighted with red as they are paid for by the projects or by contributions.

Let people know they can pay for a certain number of miles for the group. They can pay so much per mile or a larger amount for a segment of miles. The goal is to get the group members to the workcamp area, pay for the work project, food and lodging, and then get them home again. Some groups find sponsors for the travel miles and pay for the workcamp week itself through fund-raising projects.

Keeping the congregation informed, will hold their interest. You will generate excitement for the project. You'll also constantly remind people of the servant mission of the church. Those people will want to support your efforts.

Chapter Seven

Setting Up Task Forces

Involving the teenagers in the responsibilities of preparing for the workcamp pays many dividends. If group members have significant responsibility, they will invest much more in the workcamp. They will make it their own project. They will plan to succeed. Listen carefully to kids' ideas and consult them on possible alternatives for action. Give appropriate information and assist their efforts. You will serve their needs best by providing resources that will help them meet all necessary goals. The young people will make decisions, carry out planned action and do whatever work is necessary to get their jobs done.

Here are some suggested task forces:
- Steering committee;
- Budget and fund-raising projects;
- Travel and food arrangements;
- Cultural understanding;
- Skills training;
- Work-project coordination;
- Church relations and publicity;
- Preparing the youth group (building community);
and
- Post-workcamp report.

Set up responsibilities to fit your particular youth group. Depending on the size of your group, assign one young person to each task force to serve as coordinator. The coordinators can ask others to serve on their task force with them. Be sure to include one adult on each task force. If your group is small, combine the areas for which each task force is responsible.

Steering Committee

We've already discussed the importance of setting up a steering committee early in the workcamp-planning process. Avoid making decisions alone. Allow several teenagers and adults to help you. The steering committee members will clear all assignments and coordinate all plans. They will try to spread responsibilities equally among the youth group members. Steering committee members also will insist that adequate planning and preparation are done for each responsibility. The steering committee will meet periodically with the task force coordinators to see how plans are progressing. These responsibilities will guide the group's progress throughout the preparation period and the workcamp.

Budget and Fund-Raising Projects

Young people and adults on this task force will plan more details of the budget and all aspects of the fund-raising projects. They will handle all arrangements for facilities, equipment and workers' schedules. They also will coordinate with the publicity task force to advertise adequately fund raisers to the church and community.

The fund-raising task force will set goals for each project and for the total budget so all members can clearly understand the purpose and the progress of the fund raising. This task force can set up displays to chart the group's progress in raising funds.

Travel and Food Arrangements

These task force members will arrange for each night's lodging. They will choose specific types of lodging after considering all the available options.

Travel coordinators will arrange for camping and

cooking equipment, portable showers and trailers or vehicles. They will plan meals for each day either by organizing the meal preparation by group members or by setting up other food services.

Members of this task force can use special resources such as motel and campground guides and directories of churches, colleges, church camps and youth hostels. They can ask church members for information or invest in an auto club membership for help with travel planning. Many clubs' yearly fees are minimal. Shop around for the best features for the lowest price.

These task force members should research the travel route and workcamp area for possible side trips such as rafting, hiking, riding river boats, touring scenic areas and visiting theme parks or beaches. Encourage the group to select options that are affordable yet exciting. For example, many colleges allow lodging and meals for minimal or no cost. You could visit denominational colleges—these schools are most eager to "show their stuff" to high school kids.

Some groups plan singing, acting or entertainment tours to and from their workcamp area. Free lodging and fellowship dinners often can be arranged either in the hosting church or at church members' homes. You may even get acquainted with the local youth group.

Travel coordinators should prepare an itemized itinerary—complete with addresses and phone numbers— that can be handed to group members and their parents. All plans for side trips should be presented to the total youth group for suggestions and approval. The coordinators also should prepare a workcamp fact sheet that includes ideas on what clothing to bring, what to expect at the workcamp and so on. Chart 14 is a sample fact sheet that these task force members can use as a guideline.

Trip planners will determine the hours for traveling each day, along with plans for each evening. Give the planners general ideas for side trips, lodging and travel; and give them ballpark figures to begin their planning. If

Chart 14
Fact Sheet

_____
(Name of workcamp)

_____
(Location)

What to Bring
Here's a checklist of items you should bring with you to the camp.

_____ sturdy shoes or work boots	_____ work gloves
_____ hat or visor	_____ rain gear
_____ mirror	_____ camera and film
_____ Bible	_____ jacket
_____ insect repellant	_____ handkerchiefs
_____ Chap Stick	_____ sunglasses
_____ suntan lotion	_____ pen or pencil
_____ towels, washcloth	_____ sleeping bag
_____ pillow	_____ air mattress

_____ sturdy clothing: long jeans as well as shorts, socks, shirts, underwear
_____ personal toilet articles, comb, toothbrush, toothpaste, deodorant, soap
_____ plastic bags for wet or soiled clothing

Money
All needs at the camp have been covered by your camp fee. However, you'll want some spending money for snacks, etc.

Accommodations
We will stay at several churches and schools on the way to the workcamp and on the way home. During the camp we will be housed at _____ high school. We'll be sleeping on floors of classrooms—so remember your sleeping bag, pillow and air mattress.

Camp Mailing Address

_____
(Participant's name)

_____
(Name of school or camp)

_____
(Address)

_____
(City, state, Zip)

Workcamp Phone Numbers

What Will the Camp Be Like? (Add information about your own work-camp situation. Use ideas like the following.)

You'll wake up wondering why the ceiling is so far away. Then, as the cobwebs slowly drift from your mind, you'll realize that you're on the floor of Sunbright High School. You'll prepare for a day's work at the Appalachian Mountain Workcamp with the standard school picture of George Washington staring from the wall. But the smells of a hearty country breakfast will propel you toward the cafeteria where home-cooked food will strengthen you for the day ahead.

You'll pick up your sack lunch and perhaps help one of your new friends from the work crew collect the tools your crew will need. Then, you'll head for the hills!

Winding mountain roads will take you through the thick forest to a shanty that needs everything. So, you'll start with the roof and look forward to painting the place before the week ends. At least you know you'll help provide shelter from the rain and cold. Perhaps you'll fix the chimney so the hazard of fire won't be as great next winter.

You'll share your reactions to all the new experiences of the work-camp as you dig in and devour your sack lunch with your work crew. You'll laugh as you tell how much trouble you had getting your sponsor out of bed that morning.

That afternoon, you may be treated to a banjo-pickin' performance by someone living in the neighborhood. And you wonder how that sweet little ol' lady who owns the run-down house can keep smiling as if she were the happiest person in the world. You know nothing is easy for her in this place. Even her garden would take extra work and almost an acrobat to cultivate the steep hillside, which is the only place a garden could be planted.

Free time that afternoon at the high school gives you a chance to catch up on your writing, clean up a bit and just relax.

After dinner and your third trip through the serving line, you'll relax some more and then head for the evening activities. You'll learn to be a clogger from the current world-champion cloggers. You'll join in singing and clapping as local band members share some of their music. And you'll laugh at the stories flowing from a delightful lady who grew up in the coal camps. Speakers, slides and songs will fill each evening with varieties of entertainment, insight and inspiration.

Finally, you'll head for bed determined to finish that letter you started during the afternoon free time. But you'll drift off to sleep as you check for light leaks in your eyelids to the tune of your sponsor's snoring and people mumbling in their sleep.

And you can't remember if you imagined it or if the picture of ol' George smiled just a bit looking down on a room full of volunteers who wore themselves out sharing God's love with some people in Tennessee.

Permission to photocopy this chart granted for local church use only. Copyright © 1987 by Group Books, Inc., Box 481, Loveland, CO 80539.

you will be traveling a long distance to your workcamp, they can calculate approximately 400 miles per day at 50 miles per hour, resulting in eight hours of travel. They then can add time for gas stops, meals and side trips. Departure time each day should be 8 a.m. or before, to assure arriving at the lodging facility before check-in deadlines.

The task force is responsible for assigning roommates and travel companions. Switching roommates daily helps people become better acquainted. Some groups specify "friendship time" when kids travel with assigned partners for a few hours. After the friendship time, they are free to travel with anyone they choose.

Travel coordinators can organize some fun, creative activities during long hours of travel. These activities will combat boredom and can become a positive experience in building community within the group. For example, if your group will be riding in a bus, prepare a set of questions for "seat partners" to discuss: "Why did you want to come on this workcamp trip? What was your favorite fund-raising project? What are you most looking forward to during the workcamp?"

Make careful choices regarding lodging assignments, particularly when the group is staying in a motel. Try to assign one adult or mature young person to each room. Usually there will be four people to a room, so you can avoid potential problems without offending anyone.

Sometimes room assignments or sleeping area assignments can be made according to areas of responsibility. For example, breakfast cooks can sleep in a place that allows them to get up first without disturbing the whole group.

Cultural Understanding

This task force will gather information about an area's culture and plan the evening programs for during the workcamp. Books, articles, magazines and periodicals from the public library will form a basic foundation of information. The local contact person, chamber of commerce or college also may know of useful people or resources.

Search out speakers from your community to talk to your group prior to the workcamp. Pastors, social workers and sociologists who have lived in disadvantaged areas can present ideas to help the group understand the concept of poverty. Set up phone interviews with informed people from the workcamp area.

Ask the contact person, local pastors or school officials to provide names of community leaders who can interpret the culture. Arrange for these leaders to speak before the kids during the workcamp. Ask the speakers to send materials prior to the trip that the group could use for discussion and information.

Set budget guidelines for speakers fees. Once speakers understand the purpose of the workcamp, many are happy to contribute their services to help the group understand the culture.

Take great care to find quality speakers. Young people who have been working all day will doze off in a hurry if a speaker drones on and on in a boring presentation. Guide the speaker in selection of content. Few young people will be thrilled to hear a speaker explain indigenous plants. On the other hand, if a speaker brings live rattlesnakes to show the group, no one will fall asleep.

This task force can find more programming ideas in the Appendix. Evening programs can include discussions, Bible studies, games, singing, films and slide shows, as well as cultural presentations.

This task force is responsible for organizing role plays during the preparation time to help kids develop an understanding of workcamps, the culture of the area and skills in personal relationships. Role playing is the process of assigning group members the roles of people involved in real or hypothetical situations. The actors spend a few minutes "in the shoes" of their characters, exploring feelings and finding solutions for problems.

Role plays can have dramatic results. Kids practice

communicating more effectively while learning to control their feelings. Group members can give support and offer positive suggestions. Kids develop insight into situations, set goals for approaches to problems, get rid of some negative feelings and feel more confident about solving problems.

Role plays help people to experience new or unusual situations in a protected, caring group. They can try new approaches and correct mistakes without the fear of being laughed at.

Help your group members see that role plays can prepare them for workcamp situations. Role plays give them opportunities to think through possibilities that might not be seen during the pressure of an actual situation. These "rehearsals" prepare kids for actual experiences.

Follow these steps to lead role plays:

1. Describe the situation and identify the roles to be played. Choose actors for each of the roles or ask kids to volunteer. Give each actor a brief description of typical behaviors, statements or attitudes for his or her role. Use a written description or describe the role only to the corresponding actor. For instance: "Your role is an agency worker named Jeff. You always come across pretty gruff and push for all the facts about the job kids are doing on a resident's home. But you loosen up after you get to know the kids better." Or: "You are a resident whose house is being worked on. You have a negative attitude toward the work crew's efforts. But you gradually change your point of view as statements are made that make sense to you."

2. Play out the situation until the roles are presented effectively. The role play should take only a few minutes. Then stop the action and ask for responses from the actors. Invite the observers to describe what appeared helpful; to give feedback on how the process went; and to offer suggestions for improvement. It is important to offer encouragement for those actions that were productive.

3. Re-play the situation and switch roles. Try to get as many people as possible involved by repeating the role play or creating similar new ones. Let each actor tell how he or she felt during the role play. Encourage each person to share insights, possibilities and new ideas. The discussion following the role play can lead to an awareness of the problem-solving process. People will see that there are many options—not just one right way—to handle a problem or new experience.

4. Identify basic Christian values in each situation. Discuss how these values interact with and at times limit the responses that could be made. For example, a workcamper may want to yell at a lazy crew worker or bottle up feelings of frustration, but the Christian response would be to talk to the worker in a caring manner.

Consider how Jesus might have played the roles. Identify situations in Christ's life that were similar to the role plays. How did he handle strangers? poor people? negative attitudes?

If your group members don't have time to work on all the role plays together, type and make copies of the role-play descriptions and questions. Ask kids to read the situations and answer the questions.

Here is a role play that will give valuable help as you prepare your group for the workcamp. See the Appendix for more role plays.

● *Setting:* Your work site is a decaying, two-room shack. The roof leaks. Wind blows through the sides of the house. The floor is full of holes. The elderly couple living there seem very grateful for the work you are doing.

A neighbor comes by one day and protests: "These old folks have sponged off everyone for years. They never did anything for themselves. If they had half tried, they could have fixed up their place."

● *Guidelines:* Assign some kids to play work crew members who begin to question whether the elderly couple have taken advantage of them. Assign others to take the position that people don't have to earn our help. Allow a few minutes for the role play.

● *Questions:* If people haven't tried to help themselves in the past, should they be denied help now? Why or why not? Is it right for Christians to help those who seem to manipulate the kindness of others to meet their own needs? Explain. Are Christian love and compassion earned? Explain. Should those who receive Christian service be grateful? Why or why not? How would the crew have felt about fixing the elderly couple's house if they had not been appreciative?

Skills Training

The task force members can schedule a series of sessions with skilled carpenters and handymen to teach group members the basics of home repair. Kids' confidence will grow when they learn to hammer nails quickly and without bending them; saw a straight line; prepare a surface for painting; clean brushes and rollers; measure accurately; and identify types of nails to be used for each job. For everyone's benefit, safety rules and practices must be taught and tested.

Instructors can present books or handouts or sketch out the steps taken for each type of job. Books on home repair can be found in most bookstores, hardware stores and supermarkets. Chart 15 is a sample training sheet to give instructors to guide their presentations.

Encourage kids to practice the techniques at home before the workcamp. These experiences will build confidence and lead to fewer mistakes during the work projects.

This task force can use information supplied by the local contact person from the work area. The members can tailor the training and quality-control guidelines to the actual assigned projects.

Make attendance mandatory since makeup sessions create problems for the volunteer instructors. Be sure to schedule these training sessions one month or more in ad-

Chart 15
Instructor Training Outline

(This is a sample outline used by GROUP Workcamps. Use it as a
guide for preparing your own.)

Basic Workcamp Safety
  Encourage the kids to inspect the area before beginning work. Have
them look for boards with nails, broken glass, wasp nests, debris piles,
holes, loose steps or boards, electric wires, waterlines and other
potential hazards at the work site.

Basic Tool Safety and Skills
  1. Hammer—show proper techniques for hammering and removing
nails. Let everyone drive nails. Show examples of different types of
nails and what they are used for.
  2. Saw—show proper techniques for measuring and marking a
board. Demonstrate how to start the cut and how to prevent splintering
or breaking when finishing the cut. Let everyone try sawing.
  3. Screwdriver—show how to start a screw in wood. Show different
types of screws and screwdrivers used for various tasks.
  4. Electric drill—tell kids to wear safety goggles when using electric
drills. Show how to choose the proper bit and how to tighten it in the
chuck. Demonstrate drilling through wood. Remember safety aspects
such as what's under the board being drilled; where to place your free
hand; how to back out a bit; watching out for electrical cords; and so
on.
  5. Electric skill saw or circular saw—tell kids to wear safety goggles
when using these tools. Demonstrate the proper method for placing
the saw and starting a cut, positioning the hands, using assistants to
hold material being cut and finishing the cut. Also emphasize safety
factors such as taking care not to cut the electric cord and making
certain other objects are not underneath the material being sawed.
  6. Ladder—demonstrate placing a ladder so its legs are flat on the
ground and it has the proper angle of lean to the structure. Show how
to climb the ladder safely; for example, use a spotter or ask someone
to hold the ladder, especially if someone is climbing with a heavy or
bulky load.

Painting Skills
  1. Show how to put down plastic sheets or other covers to protect
shrubs, porches, furniture, etc., and demonstrate how to put masking
tape around the edges of woodwork to avoid getting paint on glass
panes.
  2. Teach how to prepare a surface for painting by removing old,
chipped or peeling paint with scrapers or wire brushes. Also, demonstrate filling in large cracks with caulk before painting.
  3. Demonstrate how to stir paint to prepare for use.

continued

Permission to photocopy this chart granted for local church use only. Copyright © 1987 by
Group Books, Inc., Box 481, Loveland, CO 80539.

Instructor Training Outline continued

4. Show how to use different types of paintbrushes for different projects.
5. Show how to use a roller to cover a large area, while preventing splattering.
6. Show how to paint the "hard-to-get-to" areas.
7. Show how to clean up brushes and rollers after finishing. (Note: We use mostly latex, a water-based paint, although enamel and oil-based paints could be used on some projects.)

Roofing Skills (Note: Meet at an old garage or shed for this element of training.)
1. Demonstrate safety on the roof. Do what can be done from ladders. Stay away from the edge. Watch out for each other. Check the roof for soft or weak spots.
2. Show how to remove old shingles or roll roofing with a flat shovel if necessary. (On most workcamp projects we nail down new roll roofing over the existing roof. No more than two layers should be covered. Three or more layers must be removed. Then, too, shingles or roll roofing may need to be removed to repair wooden decking underneath.) Emphasize that only small areas of the roof should be removed and then repaired, so that no areas of the roof are left uncovered at the day's end. It may rain!
3. Demonstrate how to measure areas to be repaired and how to measure roll roofing to cover the same areas.
4. Show how to lay out roll roofing and nail in place. Roofing nails are always used for this process. (Note: In most cases we completely cover the roof with new roll roofing.) Instruct crews to start at the bottom edge of the roof and to overlap the sheets of roofing 3 to 4 inches. Nails should be spaced 3 inches apart except on edges where they are spaced 1 inch apart. The roll roofing should overlap the edge of the roof by 1 inch on all sides.

---

vance. Calendars can be cleared or the dates protected. List this information for each training session:

- Who will conduct the training;
- Where it will be;
- What it will cover; and
- How long it will take.

Work-Project Coordination

Adult sponsors will need to carry most of the direct responsibility for this task force, since communication with the local contact person is necessary. Adults should be firm when setting up time lines for preparing cost esti-

Carpentry Skills
1. Teach how to build wooden steps using stringers. (Note: We use a formula of 7 inches of rise for every 11 inches of run.)
   a. Show how to measure, mark and cut stringers.
   b. Demonstrate how to nail on steps.
2. Show how to replace broken or rotted boards on a porch. Only replace ones that really need to be replaced.
3. Demonstrate how to install inside wallboard or dry wall.
   a. Show how to measure wallboard for the area to be replaced.
   b. Show how to cut or break wallboard after it has been measured and marked.
   c. Show how to nail the wallboard in place using dry wall nails.

Window Repair Skills
1. Teach how to remove broken glass safely. Also show how to remove old glazing or caulk if necessary.
2. Show how to install a new glass pane using push points and window glazing. (Note: We usually apply window glazing with a putty knife.)

Weatherization Skills
1. Teach how to use a caulking gun and latex caulk to caulk around windows, doors and other cracks on the house exterior.
2. Show how to install weatherstripping around doors, as well as how to install a door sweep.
3. Show how to install underpinning around a house or mobile home. (Note: If installing underpinning proves to be too expensive or impractical, perhaps workcampers could see where underpinning has been installed and closely inspect how installation is done.)

Permission to photocopy this chart granted for local church use only. Copyright © 1987 by Group Books, Inc., Box 481, Loveland, CO 80539.

mates and detailed descriptions of the projects.

Work-project coordinators will negotiate quantities of materials necessary for the project and how much time each crew will spend working. Someone with experience in home repair should identify the skills necessary for each project. These task force members will determine the success of the work projects, which provide the main purpose of the workcamp.

Church Relations and Publicity

The members on this task force will build understanding and maintain communication with support groups in the church and community. They will organize reports to parents, church organizations and the congregation through the newsletter and bulletin.

These task force members inform the community about fund raisers through community announcements, public service spots and school newspapers. They can produce posters for display through the established procedures of the church. Publicity coordinators must thoroughly promote fund-raising projects well in advance. The success of your fund raising will depend on their publicity plan.

Preparing the Youth Group

These leaders will plan ideas that build a sense of community within the group. With all the organizational efforts that will be happening, they will need to set specific times for activities that develop supportive relationships among teenagers and adults. An excellent resource for developing group cohesiveness is *Building Community in Youth Groups* by Denny Rydberg (Group Books).

Group preparation coordinators will develop general rules for participation and guidelines for acceptable behavior on the trip. They will clearly define group expectations for the outcome of the total project. Regular discussions with the youth group will generate this understanding and lead to acceptance of the expectations.

This task force clarifies procedures that will be taken if anyone breaks a major rule. Most groups outlaw sneaking out of the sleeping area at night, and all groups outlaw the use or possession of illicit drugs or alcohol. Anyone who breaks one of these rules will be sent home at the parents' expense. These rules and consequences should be identified and emphasized before the trip so there will be no surprises.

Group leaders must take immediate action on each incident of problem behavior or rule-breaking. Carefully chosen consequences for different levels of problems will maintain an atmosphere of fairness and consistency. Being late to a meeting may mean washing the dishes after a campground meal. More severe offenses will generate more severe consequences. Each group should set its own rules and consequences so that the mission of the workcamp and the reputation of the church will be strengthened by the group's behavior.

This task force will type and copy disciplinary procedures for the entire group to read and understand. Include steps for arbitration. Young people must know they will be able to state their case and be heard by group leaders. Clearly relate who will make the final decision in disciplinary matters.

This task force is responsible for making sure kids clarify and write out their own expectations about the workcamp. The youth group will experience more growth if each person has a goal. Planners provide opportunities related to those goals. For example, if someone sets a goal of learning to build steps, the crew assignments can be set up to allow that process to happen. Chart 16 is a sample form this task force could use to find out the kids' thoughts and expectations about the workcamp experience.

While setting up programs, this task force should evaluate each person's special concerns or needs. A young person who has never ventured away from home and fears becoming homesick could be assigned to call the church each day with a progress report on the workcamp. You will create a more effective group by keeping everyone as happy as possible.

Another way to prepare the group for a workcamp is to assign prayer partners. Each person has a specific personal responsibility for supporting someone else. Prayer partners should meet weekly to share their needs and thanksgivings with each other. Then their prayers will have specific purpose and meaning. You may want to keep the same prayer partners for the entire workcamp experience, or you may want to change partners periodically.

Prayer sponsors can be arranged with other groups in

Chart 16
Expectations

Please answer these questions carefully.

1. What do you expect to gain personally from the workcamp?

2. What do you expect to contribute to the workcamp experience?

3. What benefit would you like your home church to receive from your experiences at the workcamp?

4. What would you like your youth group to gain from the workcamp?

5. What would you guess God expects of you during the workcamp?

6. What would you guess the local people expect of you?

Try to picture in your mind the expectations being fulfilled. See yourself, your youth group and your church doing some new activities as a result of your experience at this workcamp. Ask God to help you accomplish what you see in your mind.

Permission to photocopy this chart granted for local church use only. Copyright © 1987 by Group Books, Inc., Box 481, Loveland, CO 80539.

the church. These task force members can ask a different group each month to pray for the workcamp. Or, they can assign specific church members to be prayer sponsors for specific workcampers. The personal element can develop powerful support for the workcamp and the people involved.

Request daily prayer support from the entire congregation. The more specific needs and concerns you share with others in the church, the more powerful your support will be. Your needs and concerns will change as the work proceeds. Continually inform the entire church about your current situation and need for prayers.

Talk with individual families about special needs or services required during the trip. Possibilities of sleepwalking, seizures, diet requirements and medication may require confidential arrangements or instructions. Some parents may express concern about the provision for sending home someone who breaks rules. If their child has been known to break rules before, work out a clear understanding between the young person, the family and the group leaders.

If there is a possibility of a death in the family from a lingering illness or condition, consider all options prior to departure so you can make decisions with a minimum of delay or difficulty. Discuss these circumstances fully to prevent major difficulties later.

Each person going on a workcamp must be healthy and strong. This task force is responsible for asking each person to have a physical and secure a physician's release to participate in the workcamp. (Parents can give the release for physical condition and work if young people have a good history of medical checkups.) Be prepared for emergencies by securing a record of shots, such as tetanus, for each person.

Physical conditioning prepares everyone for the demanding labor of work projects. Muscles will get very sore if they are not conditioned for activity before the work begins. Good physical conditioning helps ease travel pressures such as sleeping in new places. Physical conditioning enables workers to bounce back to get the job done by the end of the workcamp.

Members of this task force should encourage walking, running, swimming, stretching and calisthenics. The members also can encourage painting, roofing, hammering and sawing. These jobs help with physical fitness and they prepare kids for the work to come.

During the travel period, schedule times for walking in a city park or a public recreation area. If it is raining, a mall will offer a large covered area for a quick hike (if you can keep a leash on the die-hard shoppers in the group). Regular exercise strengthens the participants, relieves travel tension and prepares the kids for sound sleeping.

This task force is also responsible for training the group in communication skills. People who communicate effectively will accomplish more work more quickly than those who can't understand each other. Problem-solving skills also will help the group avoid the frustration of not knowing what to do when problems arise.

These coordinators can plan a series of sessions to help kids learn and practice communication and problem-solving skills. The group members will grow closer and develop needed personal resources to use when the pressure hits.

Train your group by using the training sheet for communication skills and problem-solving skills in the Appendix. Photocopy the sheet for each person to use as a reference. Several practice sessions will start your group members using the skills. Periodically remind the kids to review the skills and to continue practicing them.

Post-Workcamp Report

This task force is in charge of thinking ahead to the report for the church after the workcamp. The members select photographers well in advance and train them. Group members will enjoy reliving the trip while looking at top-quality slides. Using different types of lenses will make a big difference in your results. Ask photographers to practice during the preparatory months prior to the workcamp. Provide film for practice and for shots of the group engaged in fund-raising activities and preparatory sessions.

List the types of slides you'll need when you report to the congregation after the workcamp. Take shots of each project during each day of the workcamp. Make a list that includes each workcamper and put a check by his or her name when you capture him or her in a photo. Balance the slides to include everyone in the group and try to keep an equal number of shots of each person.

You may want to prepare a workcamp photo album along with a slide show. Learning to use higher ASA number film will prepare the photographers to take shots in low-light conditions. They then can use natural light rather than the harsher flash lighting. Ask an experienced photographer to train group photographers to provide quality slides for your report show.

This task force also is responsible for selecting interviewers to keep an audio record of the entire workcamp experience. Give interviewers tape players, tapes and microphones. Have kids interview workcampers and adult volunteers during the preparation time, during the workcamp and after the workcamp is over. Ask open-ended questions: "How did you feel prior to the workcamp? What were some of your fears? How did you feel the first day at the work site? What were your impressions of the residents? How did you feel when the work project was finished?"

Ask interviewers to record residents and agency workers during the workcamp and at the end of the week. Ask how they felt about the work crew members and the job they did. Keep lists of names, dates and places so you can identify the interviewees when you return home.

Decide how many interviews will be needed before the workcamp, so interviewers can plan their efforts. Cassette tapes are inexpensive, so lots of interviews will give you more material to use if some interviews aren't exactly what you want.

Videotaping also can be planned, but it will take more equipment and more expertise to develop a report show at the end of the workcamp. And you'll need a large screen to show a video to a large group.

Interviewers can prepare the group for the workcamp by arranging phone interviews with the agency contact person and some of the residents. Ask questions about residents' hobbies, work, families and the repair jobs needed on their homes. You'll enjoy the personal touch these interviews will add to the preparations.

Place extreme importance on preparation of the youth group. Your group members will benefit from the many sessions that will enable them to get the job done. Carefully plan your preparations to last a period of several months. Effective preparations will create a confident group that grows through the workcamp experience.

Part Three

Coordinating the Workcamp Experience

Chapter Eight
The Trip to the Workcamp

You have completed your plans and preparations. The group is excited and ready for the workcamp. The church members accept and support your efforts. They now see that you have put together a truly significant mission project. You're ready to go—almost.

Final checks before departing will save you from future problems and embarrassment. Take time to double-check thoroughly all equipment and arrangements for the trip. Follow these steps:

1. Service all vehicles and check safety. Make these checks long enough before the trip to allow plenty of time to fix any problems. Start several weeks before a trip—particularly if your vehicles are in marginal condition. A compression check of each cylinder and general engine analysis will confirm your vehicles' condition. If major problems look imminent, you will have enough time to correct them. Check the following items as well:

_____ brakes	_____ tune-up
_____ hoses	_____ oil
_____ belts	_____ radiator
_____ tires	_____ air conditioner
_____ transmission	_____ windows

2. Double-check lodging arrangements. Examine your reservations to be certain they include the correct number of rooms and the correct arrival and departure dates. Confirm the room rate and how late the rooms will be held for you.

Don't guarantee your reservations for late arrival, since something could happen that would prevent you from making it to the motel. On the day of your scheduled arrival, phone the motel to give your credit card number to hold your rooms if you will be arriving after the deadline. Be sure you record the name of the person who took your reservations and the number of rooms you requested.

3. Prepare your funds. Travelers checks will ensure safety for carrying money. Banks in nearly every city will cash these checks for you. Carrying large amounts of cash is dangerous, since losing all your money could ruin the total project.

Carry enough cash for two days of travel, along with a contingency fund for emergencies. Replenish your cash every day or two. Take a backup credit card with you to use in case of unusual circumstances. (You also can purchase food and gas with credit cards.)

4. Prepare a travel itinerary, complete with addresses and phone numbers. Copy and distribute it to church leaders, group members and parents. Be sure that parents understand your tight schedule and will support their child's involvement in the total workcamp experience. No time will be free for visits with aunts, uncles, grandparents or other relatives and friends. Such complications would only detract from the purposes and plans of the trip.

5. Use colored tape to identify tools for each owner. For example, use red tape for one person's tools, blue tape for another person's tools, and so on. Pack tools carefully in sturdy boxes. On each box, list the contents so you can quickly find any tools you may need. You will be able to organize your tool distribution more easily at the workcamp if the contents of each box are identified.

List the number of boxes you will be taking, the contents of each box, and the name and color code of each person who donated tools. Be sure that all tools are sharp and in good condition. Tools in bad condition will not be worth hauling around, since they will be of little use at the workcamp. Fix them before packing, or don't take them.

6. Collect all medical/liability release forms. Date the forms and file them alphabetically for quick access in case of emergencies. Keep them with the other important papers you'll be taking with you. Put a second copy in your first-aid kit as a backup.

7. List group members' responsibilities. Prepare copies of the responsibilities for everyone and take extras to post in handy places. Double-check with each person to confirm that all preparations are complete. Go over special assignments for the trip to be sure each person fully understands how to carry out his or her responsibilities. (The task forces described in Chapter 7 can make many of these assignments.) Review checklists for each assignment area to see if the equipment or supplies are ready. For example, bring window cleaner and rags for the people assigned to wash vehicle windows. Here are areas of responsibility for the trip:

● *Vehicle inspectors.* These people must completely check the vehicles at the start and end of each day. At the beginning of the day, the tires, radiator and engine are cool, so they can be checked easily and accurately. If you must add fluids or air, it's always best to do so when vehicles are cold. An oil check will be more accurate because all the oil will be resting in the bottom of the oil pan.

At the end of each day, check the vehicles for problems that will need correction before departure the next day. Vehicle inspectors may forget about their assignment in their desire to dive into a swimming pool or cool off in an air-conditioned motel room. But the sooner problems are discovered, the sooner they will be fixed. It only takes a few minutes to completely inspect the vehicles.

During each gas stop, checks must again be made to ensure that no problems are developing. A nail may be causing a slow leak, and you can save a tire by catching the problem before much air is lost. Clean windows promote safety. At every stop, remove all grime and bug remains. Windows must be completely clean, particularly toward the beginning or end of the day when the sun could be shining directly into the driver's eyes.

● *Personal inventory facilitator.* This person reminds the group at appropriate times to do an attitude check. Self-awareness will keep grumpiness from surfacing. Focusing attention, even for a short time, on personal expectations of the present day will create a positive attitude in the group.

Periodically schedule group discussions. Early in the trip, expectations may be more easily discussed. After the second or third day, attitudes may need more attention. Prepare some community-building activities that will emphasize positive attitudes and expectations. For example, the facilitator could have each young person discuss with a partner the best thing that happened to him or her that day.

The person responsible for this area could prepare by reading a peer counseling book such as *Friend to Friend* by Larry Keefauver and J. David Stone (Group Books). This simplified approach to helping friends through problems could make a difference in dealing with deteriorating attitudes in the group.

● *Photographers.* Slides of the group should include many travel experiences. Be alert for good shots you can take while traveling or at rest stops and during visits to attractions. Again, use a checklist to ensure that everyone gets his or her picture taken.

● *Journal writer.* Select a good writer to make notes and compose an account of the interesting, humorous and unusual experiences of each day. This person will describe each day's experiences and add special entries to spice up the journal. Periodically, this person should interview group members for experiences they want to remember.

Take care not to allow sarcasm or put-downs to be part of the journal. Everyone deserves the right to be proud of the written record of the workcamp experience. When you return home, read the final draft of the journal.

Whenever a particular entry is questionable, consult the people involved to determine what they will accept as a journal entry. Make adjustments in the journal, and then make copies for all workcampers. You could even put a copy in the church library as a record of the youth group's mission trip.

• *Treasurer.* This person must keep all receipts of all expenses during the trip. Keeping detailed records enables you to give clear explanations of expenses in case questions or problems arise when you return from the trip. List and total daily expenses.

You can buy a travel-expense book at an affordable price. This book makes everything look professional and it eases the process of keeping records.

Make a daily check with budgeted expenses. You will feel relieved if everything goes as expected. If not, you can make adjustments quickly before bigger problems happen.

• *Lodging supervisor.* This person prepares a list of facilities with phone numbers and confirmation numbers. He or she arranges lodging facilities in order of use. He or she also indicates the method of payment on the list, so whoever is paying bills will know what to do at check-in or checkout time.

Check notes for reservation deadlines each day. If the group is behind schedule, you may need to call to reserve your rooms for late arrival. In case of major delays, the steering committee will need to meet to decide whether or not to proceed to the reserved motel or campground.

• *Equipment supervisor.* This person lists all equipment and then double-checks it as it's packed to be sure nothing is left behind. Space for equipment may be limited, so load equipment into vehicles one or more days ahead of departure. You can solve problems with space more effectively with a day or two available to make other arrangements.

Take time to inspect all equipment. Set up tents to check for holes, rips or rot. You may immediately see a need for more tent stakes or extra ropes. Try out the cooking equipment to see if it is operational and to get special instructions in case no one can make it work.

Describe the condition of the equipment. Make notes of any damage existing at the time of receiving the equipment. Discuss with the owner any questions or problems immediately.

● *Daily prayer and spiritual growth coordinator.* A spiritual growth coordinator plans at least one prayer time each day. He or she can focus the group's attention on mission by reading servanthood scriptures. Discussion questions can help the group concentrate when everyone is tired and having trouble focusing on the scripture or the experiences of the day. For example, this person can read about Jesus feeding the 5,000 (Matthew 14:13-21). He or she can ask questions such as: "How do you think Jesus felt prior to this tremendous task? If he was tired at the end of the day, how did he get the energy to continue his work? How can we energize ourselves for our mission?"

This person looks for ways to catch people giving God's love to each other and to others outside the group. Calling attention to their giving can help group members identify God's action in their lives. When this process happens a few times, others will be able to do the same thing. The group can get caught up in the fun and excitement of looking for God's presence every day.

"Down" times can be a source of spiritual growth as well. Relying on the Spirit of Christ for strength and guidance will help when personal spirits drag. Looking at the positive side of down times can be one of the most powerful experiences for recognizing the power of God's love.

● *First-aid supervisor.* The person in charge of medical treatment must have fresh and adequate supplies ready. Try to assign a person who has been officially trained in first aid and has a current certificate. You also will need first-aid pamphlets, books and kits, particularly if you will be dividing into several crews for the work projects.

Pack a first-aid kit in a readily available place in each vehicle. Pack special medications that must be refrigerated with the food, or separate them in a cooler. Coordinate special instructions for any individual's condition or possible needs.

● *Tunes coordinator.* Because of the community-building aspects of a youth group trip, insist that kids leave personal tape players and radios at home. People who are constantly plugged in to their private listening world will not experience much companionship during the trip.

Prior to the trip, the tunes coordinator asks everyone to make requests for specific albums and favorite songs. The youth group will need to decide if some music will be off-limits for the trip.

At predetermined times during the trip, the tunes coordinator plays the selected music. Use a rotating schedule of tunes to assure fairness in playing all music equally. Give drivers a license to kill the music whenever it interferes with their concentration.

The tunes coordinator also will regulate the volume level. This function will demand a diplomatic person. Volume decisions may be required at any time because of headaches or a special need to talk.

● *Crisis management committee.* Assign a group of people (possibly the steering committee) to take charge of any problems that occur. Travel problems such as breakdowns, getting lost, possessions left behind, illness of one of the travelers or getting caught in a traffic accident can erupt at any time. Before the trip, discuss crisis guidelines. Brainstorm every possible problem and solution to help prepare this group for the unexpected.

Interpersonal problems may take on crisis proportions. Outline the steps to take for crisis management; for example, steps to take when kids break rules. Clarify the method of making a final decision so the group understands the process. Remember, anticipated problems will be handled more smoothly than completely unexpected ones. Never ignore potential problems. Keep in mind what steps you'll take if a particular crisis occurs.

You may need to talk with people who have a history of problems before the trip. Discuss possible difficult situations and how the problems will be handled. Develop a mutual understanding without bringing the total group into the conversation.

Arrange special support partners for any person who may need daily attention. A series of assigned traveling partners can keep an individual on track who may have difficulty with self-control or judgment. By sharing these responsibilities, you will obligate no one person throughout the trip to be the helping person.

Pre-travel interviews with people who may have special requests or needs will help prepare for extra attention during the trip. Make notes of special requests or concerns. List daily reminders of these concerns, and place them on your personal calendar for attention during the trip.

● *The steering committee.* These leaders will need to plan daily meeting times. They can discuss observations about special needs or the general climate within the group. They'll need to take action or make decisions before the group's daily discussions or prayer time. Responding to the changing atmosphere within the group will be a daily challenge.

Teachable moments may happen daily. Teachable moments are times when a meaningful truth can be applied. For example, a gas station attendant may be rude at one of your refueling stops. Discuss the situation with the kids. Point out how Christians need to be helpful and positive because we reflect Christ's love. Look for special opportunities to apply scripture and prayer. Develop a plan of action for responding to these valuable times.

The steering committee can help others anticipate the workcamp by playing a discussion game called "What If?" A steering committee member could write each of the following questions on separate 3×5 cards. Each person receives a card and reads the question. He or she responds to the question, then others can say what they'd do in the situation. You can play this discussion game while traveling, during evening devotions or while sitting around a campfire.

1. What if, on the first day out, your crew cannot locate the house you've been assigned?

2. What if your crew arrives at a work site and you discover the residents have moved or are not at home?

3. What if the instructions for the project are unclear?

4. What if there are no materials available to complete the project as it is written up? What if the wrong materials are at your site?

5. What if a particular aspect of the job seems too dangerous, too difficult or beyond your crew's abilities?

6. What if tools are lost or broken?

7. What if your crew needs more materials or tools?

8. What if a work crew member becomes ill or is injured?

9. What if it rains?

10. What if you are instructed to tear off old roofing materials?

11. What if someone forgets his or her sack lunch?

12. What if you encounter vehicle problems?

13. What if there are problems with residents?

14. What if there are discipline or behavior problems within the crew?

15. What if the residents make requests for repairs beyond those written up for the project, or your crew sees additional work that needs to be done?

16. What if neighbors want you to work on their house?

17. What if your crew finishes early?

18. What if there are materials left over when you finish your project?

8. Commission the group by the congregation.
As a final public statement that the workcamp is a *con-*

gregational mission (not just the youth group), commission the group during worship on the Sunday prior to departure. Ideally, the entire worship service centers on the value of mission and service in the name of Christ. Litanies of dedication, special prayers for safety and wisdom and other acts of worship communicate to all why the group is embarking on a mission of service and love. At some point in the service, ask the young missionaries to come forward. Then do some kind of special commissioning. Your church's traditions may determine the form of this service. This commissioning will help young people feel "sent forth" by their congregation.

9. Take off! Once you double-check equipment and arrangements and assign responsibilities to kids, you can leave for your trip. An early start the first morning works best, since most people will be too excited to sleep. For a long day of driving, schedule relief drivers to share the load. Ask kids to bring sack lunches for the first day to save money and time.

Never plan to drive all night when going on a workcamp. People are thrown off schedule too much, and fatigue and illness become much more probable. A regular schedule makes everything better.

You will be launching a mission as representatives of your church, so a brief celebration of worship and thanksgiving is a must. Instruct kids to get their stuff on the vehicles and then send them and the parents to the sanctuary. In the sanctuary, consecrate your strength and energy to the mission. Ask the group members to pray for the workcamp and for safety in travel. Ask parents to support the group's actions and efforts with their prayers throughout the time you are away. Ask for God's special blessing on your plans and efforts so his love will be powerful in all that you do.

Allow a time to share briefly the hopes and expectations for the trip. If you have a theme for the workcamp, restate the theme and the scriptures that support it. One appropriate scripture is Isaiah 40:31: "But those who hope in the LORD will renew their strength. They will soar on wings like eagles; they will run and not grow weary, they will walk and not be faint.''

Offer a closing prayer for God's strength and guidance throughout the trip.

Make a final check for sack lunches and kids' belongings. Then load up the workcampers and take off for your mission!

Chapter Nine

At the Workcamp

When you arrive at the workcamp location, you'll finally spring into action after hours of traveling. If you camp with tents and cook your meals, you'll face the task of setting up. Here's where your planning, training and preparation will pay off.

The following are points you need to know about being at the workcamp:

1. Setting up a "tent city" will demand careful choices. Selecting the best spot for tents and cooking will make a difference if inclement weather sets in. Set up your tents on sloped terrain and away from older trees that could lose limbs during a windstorm. Locate the cooking area where it will be sheltered in case of rain. Use your most experienced people to make these decisions.

One year, we had Carl supervise setup. Carl had earned an Eagle Scout award, so the group automatically appointed him "mayor" of the workcamp's tent city. Since much time had elapsed between the training sessions and the trip, he reminded everyone how to prepare the sites and put up the tents.

Carl inspected the completed setup and then reinspected the tents twice each day to make sure the group had tightly staked each tent and prepared for any foul weather. Carl's extra work and care paid off when our well-trenched tents, located on gently sloping ground, survived a two-hour thunderstorm.

The young people and adult sponsors respected his

expertise. Everyone admired his calm, easygoing manner
as he helped the more inexperienced campers. We all felt
we had special knowledge and training when Carl was
through with us.

If you will be sleeping in other types of arrangements,
your task will be simpler. Prior to moving in, inspect all
sleeping quarters to protect your group from suspicion or
accusation in case there is already some damage to the facility. Someone may blame your group for the damage if
you don't call attention to it before you use the facility.
Always confirm in writing the condition of the rooms.
State the date and the name of the person representing the
facility whom you told about the damage. Specifically state
that you found the facilities damaged when you arrived.

Inspect all restrooms and showers to ensure sanitary,
safe and healthy conditions. Assign a cleanup crew to sani-
tize the area if those responsible for the facility can't or
won't do the work. Even an old facility can be cleaned
and sanitized.

Be sure to carry or purchase plenty of bug spray for
cockroaches, ants and flying insects, just in case they're
crawling all over the area.

If you're preparing your own meals, cooks should
start early with meal preparation so growling stomachs
won't distract the neighborhood. Keep some backup cans
of food in a handy place just in case a complete disaster
unfolds in the kitchen.

If you will be eating in restaurants during the workcamp, survey the participants for their preferences. The
budget limits may rule out some of their favorites, unless
you've made special plans for a better meal on occasion.
Look for novelty restaurants that represent the unique
food of the area. Always provide a variety of food for
those with special needs.

Assess any special safety and security considerations in
your living area. If group members want to venture out in
the evening for touring or special activities, take precautions for security. During the daytime when everyone is

working, you will face the same concern. Take valuable equipment with you whenever everyone leaves. Anything that can be carried away faces possible change of ownership. If you have any concern about the safety of your equipment, make special arrangements for some kind of security monitor.

2. Strategy meetings with the local contact person and other leadership will demand your attention when you arrive. Check immediately on the current status of the work projects. Have materials been delivered to the sites? If not, you will need to make a major effort to prepare the projects for the first workday.

If there are too many projects for you to inspect, assign several teams to examine the projects. Take a copy of the project description (see Chapter 5) and check all items listed. Look for safety concerns at each site. Make sure someone will be at the residence while the work is being done. On this first visit, you also can start the important process of building a relationship with the residents who have opened their homes to your crews.

Make final notes about needed items at each project. Look for small, essential items such as screws or nails. Crews will be frustrated if these items are missing. (One thing that frustrates people even more is the resident being absent when the crew first arrives.)

3. Meet with the total group after you complete the inspections. Go over all guidelines for quality work and emphasize safety procedures. Remind the crews not to take tape players and radios to the work area. Residents and neighbors may resent the volume or type of music the group would play. Listening to music can prevent conversations from happening naturally during the day. Challenge the group members to find ways of relating without imposing their music on the situation.

Remind the group about proper use of tools. Using the wrong tool in a certain job will quickly break the tool or render it useless. Be sure kids understand the importance of cleaning tools after each use and protecting the surrounding area if they are painting or doing anything that could damage something nearby.

Remind workcampers to prepare each procedure carefully before actually doing it. Give advice such as: "Measure twice and cut once." "Clean all surfaces and remove all loose material before painting." "Start a project right, and it will end right." This advice will prevent many potentially expensive blunders. Ask kids to take special care while working around windows. Glass can break very easily if handled incorrectly.

Extra care and double-checking will create top-quality workmanship. Ask the group to support each other with reminders to be safe and careful throughout the work project.

4. Use the evening before the work begins for spiritual, emotional and crew preparation. Focus the group's attention on possible friendships that can be developed with people from the local community. Ask kids to listen carefully and exercise courtesy when talking with residents.

Divide the kids into the crews you have assigned for each project. Have each crew designate members to be responsible for these areas throughout the week:

● *Breakmaker*—This person decides when the daily breaks and lunch time will be taken. This person also is in charge of picking up the cans of pop for breaks every morning after breakfast, taking them to the work site, and finding a cold place for them.

● *Devotion leader*—This person is the leader of the daily work crew devotions. The devotion leader must sense how well the crew is operating and interacting. Insight from scripture and prayer time can guide the crew's time together. He or she should ask the crew for suggestions of how to use different spiritual strengths to serve well and build Christian friendship.

● *Crew reporter*—This person will meet daily with agency workers to discuss progress, problems, etc. He or she will also report immediately upon return from the work project if more materials and tools are needed. Before leaving the work site, he or she should obtain task information from the work coordinator to determine exactly what size, how many and what kind of materials and tools are needed.

● *Quartermaster*—This person will make sure his or her work crew has all necessary tools to carry out the daily tasks. He or she will go with the crew reporter to help pick up the tools and to inventory them. At the end of the day this person should meet with the work coordinator to decide what tools to add or delete for the next day.

● *Work coordinator*—This person obtains daily task information from the agency workers (or person in charge of the entire workcamp). He or she also clarifies each person's skills, decides who will do each job and checks progress. If more help is needed, he or she should ask crew members if they would like help from another crew to complete the project by the end of the week. If more help is needed, this person tells the crew reporter to present the request in his or her daily report. Each day before leaving the work site, the coordinator should check to see that the quartermaster is returning all tools and that all tools are clean.

After assigning crew roles and responsibilities, celebrate God's love through a special worship service. Focus kids' intentions on being God's servants so that their quality of serving will be the best it can be.

Remind the kids that church members will be praying for them throughout the week. Say: "Our time of work combines a time of celebration. God has given this opportunity to be his hands, his arms and his feet. We have the privilege of being the love of God as we carry out a mission of service in the name of his Son, Jesus Christ. Celebrate the opportunity!"

The short service should close with a special time of prayer and consecration of each person's energies. Ask kids to pray for spiritual support for the work and responsibilities of the mission project.

5. Physical preparation demands a good night's sleep. Ask the group members to be considerate of everyone's need for sleep, even if they are too excited to sleep themselves. Out of respect for others, they can lie quietly in bed if they're not sleepy.

Be clear that the lights-out time also includes a time to be totally quiet. Talking after lights out will create a problem for those who need to sleep. The day starts early, and much hard work will be required. Ask someone in each room to give an "end-of-the-day" prayer at lights-out time, so kids will open their hearts to God and close their mouths for sleep.

6. Beginning the first day's work will challenge and excite everyone. Challenges remind us of our need for spiritual strength, particularly when we face something new and different. Each day, crews should remind each other of the spiritual dimension of their work. A brief scripture reading and discussion along with prayers are appropriate during a break or at lunch time. Though brief, these times set the mood and the framework for Christian service.

Each person will profit from answering these questions: "Why are we here? Who is supporting us? What do we need to accomplish? How do we feel about this opportunity?" During the middle of each day, each crew should assess progress: "How are things going? What needs to happen this afternoon? Do any problems need attention?"

The crew members also can look ahead to the evening session with the total group as a time for sharing their experiences. They can report actions or insights that connected with their devotion or with the workcamp's overall goal. Whenever they see God working in their crew, they have something important to report to the rest of the group. Acts of kindness or helpfulness done by a worker, special appreciation shown by a resident and special Christian insight within the work crew all represent different expressions of God's love.

Not every crew will need to report—just the ones who have had a special insight or deeper understanding of the meaning of the day's scripture. Reports must reflect the spiritual dimension of the workcamp, not just a sharing of funny stories. Christian insight will be lost if socializing takes over.

The reports may reveal something like Steve's experience. He played football and saw himself as strong and tough. At the work site, he struck up a friendship with a little guy named Danny, the son of a local resident. At first, they got along very well. All the crew members knew Danny and Steve were developing a special relationship.

After a couple of days, Steve felt disturbed by Danny's sketchy description of how he had received the scars on his arms and legs. The stories seemed to revolve around his daddy. But Danny avoided any specifics about what had happened to him.

One afternoon some confusion broke out among the workcampers. Steve spouted off in anger. After cooling down, he looked for Danny and found him hiding way up in a tree in the back yard. Danny had seen Steve's angry outburst and had run away to hide. When Steve tried to coax him down, Danny spit on him and screamed for him to go away.

The friendship withered. Danny feared that Steve, who was big like his daddy, would get angry and hit him. Danny kept his distance the rest of the day. Steve cried himself to sleep that night.

The next evening, Steve shared how much his insight and understanding about anger had grown. He learned how powerful an expression of anger can be and how important it is to choose when to express anger. He also realized that circumstances sometimes make a friendship hard to build. He could see his need for God's help much more clearly when he realized that some things were beyond his ability to handle.

Afterward, Danny and Steve talked about the experience and why each of them reacted as they did. Their friendship deepened as a result of the conversation.

By discussing the experiences of the different work crews, all workcampers can grow closer together, even though they work in different places. They contribute to the growth and understanding of the other crews by offering their experiences and the special ways God made himself known that day.

7. Set up an easy way to distribute tools and materials. The quartermaster for each crew should check out the necessary tools for his or her project and take them to the site. A "tool depot" will make this process possible. Collect all tools in one location. Gather one box for each crew and assign each crew a number. Number the boxes so you can match them to the corresponding crews. Fill each crew's box with tools it will need. This process can be completed the day before the projects begin so that toolboxes are waiting for the crews when they are ready to depart to the sites.

If there is a big demand for certain tools, crews may need to take fewer numbers of tools with them. A crew can assign different jobs to different people so that everyone will not need the same tool. Tools also can be shared among crews if they are close to one another. Schedule tools for distribution to a certain crew in the middle of the week after another crew has completed its need for those tools.

Each day, have the crews return their toolboxes to the tool depot. Rearrange tools as necessary to provide the right tools for each crew the following day. Crews should report to the toolroom coordinator each afternoon after the work is finished, to let him or her know the status of their project and whether or not they need fewer, the same or more tools. Tool coordination flows more smoothly if your crews work closely together. Careful site selection will affect this process.

Make every effort to keep crews supplied with necessary materials. If their vehicle has enough room, material can be transported to the work site by the crew members.

If it has enough workers, the local agency may be able to deliver materials.

Check your materials budget each time you purchase supplies. Compare your daily purchase totals with the total budget. This procedure will keep you aware of your spending level. Avoid adding more repairs to the projects and overspending, since every project will have more work that needs to be done. Complete repairs and remodeling would go beyond the scope of the assigned project. Many homes would require total rebuilding if everything were to be fixed. Limited repairs will be of significant help, however, so keep the crews looking on the positive side of what they are doing rather than looking at what still needs to be done.

Keep talking with participants about the requests homeowners make for more repairs. Your budget could not possibly cover every problem in all the homes you are helping. Help workers and residents understand the realistic limits of the workcamp.

8. On the first day, review the purpose of your mission with the total group. Ask the crews to review the special concerns of the area and of the families with whom they will be working. They need to maintain sensitivity to the residents' circumstances.

Challenge the workers to make a good first impression on the people they meet. Remind the group members to be courteous and sensitive to the feelings of residents and the neighbors around the project. Remind them of the role plays they practiced and of the importance of thinking about others' reactions and impressions.

Careful and sensitive offerings of friendship will create opportunities for relationships that will grow throughout the week. Ask the young people to be friendly without being pushy.

Remind each crew to organize its time for the day. Plan breaks about midway during the morning work period and the same for the afternoon. Review responsibilities for each person so everyone knows who to ask for help or decisions in a certain area. Plan for progress reviews at midday and at the end of the day. Usually during cleanup time, the crews can evaluate their progress. If one person must do several things, encourage that person to use a checklist to be sure everything gets done.

Each day, assign a person to run any necessary errands. Be careful not to assign someone who is crucial to the work project. Key people will carry too much responsibility at the work sites to allow them to leave.

Remind the crews to absorb all the experiences of the day as possibilities for discovering something new. Even problems can lead to new understanding. Many young people have defeated personal insecurities as a result of experiences that happened accidentally at a workcamp.

Anne had discovered her diabetes when she was 7. Her life since that time revolved around treating her condition. She had to give herself an insulin injection every morning. She lived with a nagging fear that her friends would find out she was "different." She wanted to keep her special need a secret.

At the workcamp, only the adults knew what she was doing each morning. She would slip into the bathroom after everyone else was outside the building and give herself an insulin injection. Things worked well all week until she forgot her shot one day. The crew was traveling about 30 minutes from the base camp and had to turn around to retrieve her insulin.

Anne churned inside. She not only had created a time problem, but now the whole group knew she had diabetes. No one said much while Anne raced into the building to get her syringe and medicine. She gritted her teeth and boarded the van, determined not to cry when everyone made fun of her.

The group gasped with fascination as Anne went through the entire procedure of preparing the shot, cleaning an area for the injection and then sticking herself with the needle. Everyone was impressed, especially the boys who thought they were pretty tough. They confessed they wouldn't even think about giving themselves a shot.

During the rest of the trip, the group learned about diabetes and how it can be controlled for a reasonably active and healthy lifestyle. Anne also gained a new self-image as someone with strengths, rather than someone with a secret problem.

Anne became an encourager in the group when someone would say, "I could never do that!" She would answer, "You can do almost anything if your life depends on it." And people knew she spoke from experience.

Personal growth can happen in many ways, so remind everyone to keep an open mind to see what God is leading him or her to understand.

9. Directing the workcamp is a functional responsibility one person will carry. The youth minister or an adult sponsor can carry this responsibility. Or someone with home repair or construction experience could take over the assignment if that arrangement works for your group. When someone other than the youth minister is the workcamp director, be careful to write out a detailed job description. Maintain clear understanding of the responsibilities. Explain the division of responsibility and authority to the youth group members so they will know who to approach with various types of problems.

If there are many crews working in several different areas, the workcamp director could function as a coordinating director by checking with the various crews during the day. If immediate needs emerge, the director can authorize and initiate action to resolve the situation.

The work director also could function as a director of encouragement. While visiting the sites, he or she could look for ways to encourage positive attitudes and quality workmanship. Stay attentive to the mood of the crews and the group in general. Look for ways to prevent a sense of boredom or drudgery. Distribute surprises to the crew such as fruit, candy or other special little treats.

If someone runs out of work while others are still busy, encourage him or her to find creative ways to be helpful. Even painting a mailbox can be more fun than sitting around. Add some special decorations to the paint job if there is some artistic talent in the group.

Make a positive effort to affirm the process of working together to finish a project. Brag about team spirit or cooperation within the crew. Give positive feedback whenever you catch someone doing a good job.

Quality control influences every aspect of the workcamp. You will want the best possible experience for the young people, residents and local agency. Watching everyone's morale will take special effort.

The workcamp director will need to resolve conflicts as various value systems press for their particular interests. The agency will want a perfect job. Residents will want the whole house refurbished. Tired workers will want a break.

The director will need to find the middle ground between the various value systems and create a common ground of satisfaction. Set reasonable limits at the beginning of the planning stage and then restate them periodically throughout the project. With clear goals and limitations, fewer complaints will surface and more satisfaction will be achieved.

Write out all goals, expectations, budget amounts and responsibilities so that fuzzy memories will not create problems after the project begins. Refer to those written statements to establish an understanding when conflicts occur.

Maintaining positive attitudes and high morale within the work crews will provide a foundation for conflict management. Community-building activities in the evenings will keep the group members connected with their common goals and interdependent functions. Spiritual growth during worship times will keep the group open to God's Spirit of love.

Use care cards as a way to affirm workcampers. Give each person a Manila envelope and a pencil. Have kids each write their name on an envelope and hang it in a central location. Always keep 3×5 cards and pencils by the envelopes. Each day encourage kids to write affirmations to each other on 3×5 cards and place them in the corresponding envelopes. Since care cards are limited to positive statements of care for others, they help build positive attitudes and self-esteem within the group.

Care cards work best when each person fills them out each day. At least one card for each work crew member sets the standard. This foundation of caring keeps people looking for ways to care about others. The process of writing personal messages gives kids an opportunity to express their caring attitude directly—but not too directly.

10. Adults working with the crews play a special role. Because of their experience and maturity, adults furnish the stability of the work crew. However, their special opportunity lies in coaching the young people to carry out their responsibilities and make decisions. Adults must let young people take major responsibility for their assigned tasks.

Adults who function as dictators or generals in a work crew create resistance among the kids. Adults can monitor progress, make suggestions when asked, and model good work, but they should not push young people aside and do the work themselves.

Young people will grow the most when adults ask questions, listen carefully and make suggestions. Of course, if safety, injury or damage is a possibility, adults must take charge and use their more mature common sense to prevent any hazardous activity.

Allowing young people an opportunity to serve can brighten their lives. Sometimes, no one suspects that certain young people have special skills or abilities.

Trudie surprised everyone as a contributor to a workcamp. No one suspected she had a special skill, because no one knew her. The project was at a ranch in Montana, and part of the crew's job was to help with the animals.

Trudie's knowledge flashed on the scene like a meteor. She quickly became the crew's adviser. She handled the cattle and horses so well that the guys were impressed. Her example pushed other girls to drop their hesitancy about working with animals. Her spark ignited the crew into an experience of a lifetime as the crew helped round up the cattle and brand them in the corral.

When the group members discussed their experiences and bragged about Trudie's knowledge, she revealed that she was planning for a career in veterinary medicine. The miracle of being in the right place with the freedom to take responsibility brought Trudie solidly into the youth group. Her friends formed a higher regard for her, and her confidence grew.

Adults who allow people like Trudie to take charge use their maturity to refrain from controlling the group. When adults relinquish total control, God's Spirit works within the kids to complete the project.

Prepare the adults within the work crews to respond to emergencies. Injuries need an experienced response and calmness from someone who has possibly seen the same or similar problem. Train the adults to carefully follow established first-aid instructions. Encourage them to respond in a manner appropriate to whatever injury or emergency happens. Their adult maturity will set the tone for the kids' reactions. Doing too much or too little can be a big problem with injuries and first aid, therefore adults may offer the best resource for the crew.

Some crews may include trained and certified young people who know more about first aid than anyone else. If so, adults will take a back seat and give support as an appropriate response.

11. Continue to interact daily with the local contact person. This communication is essential to a successful workcamp. Progress reports from the work crews and the local supervisors at the end of each day will maintain perspective for all the leadership. Each day, all agency quality-control supervisors should convey any project problems or evaluations. Any crews needing special advice or assistance will need supervisors to help them complete the job correctly.

Daily progress assessments help determine whether you can finish all the projects on time. Some crews may need more assistance to meet their goal. Or you may need to call on an expert supervisor from the agency staff to assist a group that faces unusual problems.

One crew suddenly needed outside help. It had started putting a new floor on a porch when the concrete pillars began sinking into the ground. It took some expert guidance and two feverish days of work to lay a new foundation that wouldn't sink. Then the crew worked two more days with two additional crews to complete the project.

Workcamp leadership must make daily decisions to keep the projects on schedule and to ensure that the work will be done. Because of the importance of finishing the projects, you may need to consider using the contingency fund to pay for extra help. But do this *only* as a last resort.

Young people will benefit most from completing their projects during the workcamp. Because of this important factor, adding expert help during the workcamp makes the most sense if the project falls behind schedule. Occasionally, groups have hired workers locally to complete parts of a job after the workcamp ends. Sometimes agency personnel will arrange to work weekends or after hours at reduced rates to complete projects. Finishing the projects always remains a major priority and should be accomplished if at all possible.

If crews finish their projects early, they can be assigned to projects needing more help. Make plans for crews that have unique skills or fast workers to help with special jobs toward the end of the week.

If local agency workers act lethargic about the projects or simply fall apart in their organizing, you will need to take positive action to complete the projects. The young people will want to complete whatever they've started. Agency people who don't worry about progress because they know they will complete the work after you've gone have missed the point. The feelings of the young people are a top priority!

When working with a local agency, you may have to be assertive to make your point. You have traveled many miles and invested significant time and money in order to complete some projects. You did not invest all that time and money just to work for a while. Your purpose has never changed. You accepted the challenge of a mission to complete your work projects for the benefit of residents and workcampers.

Residents also expect their work to be completed as announced from the beginning of the week. You may need to ask local lumber companies to stay open longer in order to purchase materials after the crews have reported back from the work sites.

As soon as you recognize a potential problem with completing the projects, set daily goals that will allow you to finish. Ask the agency for suggestions and resources. Talk to the crews about spending a few more hours each day to get the job done. Don't wait until the last day to take action.

12. There will be special problems at the workcamp. Weather problems need advance planning. If rain hits like a monsoon, what will you do? Plan at least part of every project to have indoor work such as painting. Always plan to do indoor work at the end of the week so you'll have work to do even if it rains the last day. If rain continues beyond the time the crews have finished with their indoor projects, you can plan backup projects such as painting school hallways or classrooms, community buildings or agency facilities. Again, make arrangements to complete the projects after the workcamp, if something prevents your crews from getting the jobs done.

Extremely hot weather may force you to adjust your schedule. You may choose to work early in the morning and quit work by noon. One workcamp in Wichita Falls, Texas, worked through a heat wave of daily 116-degree temperatures. Crews adjusted their schedules to start work at 4 a.m. each day. They worked until noon and then retreated to their air-conditioned living quarters or went swimming. As a result, the only medical problem during the workcamp involved a worker who caused her own exhaustion by running up the steps at a water slide.

If projects are delayed because of weather, reset your goals in order to complete the projects. Consider longer hours, more help from local church, agency or community volunteers. You can also evaluate each project so that the most important parts of the job will be done first. Take whatever measures you can to complete the work. The example you set for young people will be worth whatever it takes.

Problems with local troublemakers can disrupt your experience at any level. Talk with your local contact person to consider possible problems and how to handle them. As a general rule, local people handle local problems best. Find resource people in the community who will consult with you if problems occur.

Local guys may appear and show interest in the girls in the group. If you can have contact with a high school teacher, counselor or principal, ask that person to be present early in the week to talk with local people. He or she can explain the nature of the program and request that the workcamp be left to pursue its mission. Local leaders' involvement and cooperation usually take care of problems.

The most difficult situation arises when local community leaders misunderstand or confuse your program with a government program that works with juvenile delinquents. This kind of misdirected rumor can cause many problems in the community. You'll need good local support to clear up the misunderstanding. Local media can interview you and some of the residents to clear up the misunderstanding. Ask local pastors to help. They may exert just the right influence to straighten out a problem.

Invite community leaders to your work projects and

evening programs. They quickly will find a different picture from the rumors they heard.

Problems with workcampers can also disrupt the flow of the group. Conflict happens in every family, and a workcamp group quickly becomes a type of family while living and working together. Facing the conflict head-on generally works best, since the direct approach will resolve the problem most quickly.

Conflict often revolves around perceptions of who is doing the most work. Adults will need to explore possibilities for emphasizing the success of the less capable workers, while helping the more capable workers bask in an internal satisfaction gained from helping others learn new jobs. Paint new images of success in the minds of young people by showing them how to look at an experience the way God would see it.

Personality conflicts may break out at a workcamp. The strain of work and living in close quarters grows throughout the week. Resolving these conflicts completely is beyond the scope of a workcamp. However, focusing on acceptance for a certain amount of time challenges a young person within reasonable guidelines. Even limited control of a conflict will induce confidence. The young person will gain experience in controlling personal feelings and behaviors. Reinforcing a young person's growth in this area will propel him or her to take charge of his or her life.

New bonds of friendship may spring from experiencing the helpfulness of someone who used to seem unlikable. Seeing another person in a new way can open doors that were not even considered in the past. The evening discussions will stretch young people's growth in these areas of interpersonal conflict.

Learning to lean on Jesus for help will splash a fresh spirit on teenagers. Even the adults may need a spiritual boost after arriving at the brink of personal control. When the stress of a workcamp hits, young people often see prayer as a necessity and not as just "going through the motions" in a religious way.

Looking at problems that probably will occur at a workcamp points to the need for breaking the pattern of work in the middle of the week. Working a half day at midweek will nudge the group members into a change of pace. They'll find a renewed perspective and a spark of energy that will put the light back in their smile. This brief holiday can be used for relaxation in whatever form best suits the group.

Some will want active tension-relieving recreation. Others will want to do laundry to relieve pressure and halt their worries about dirty clothes. Others will want to sleep or write a few letters and enjoy a time to withdraw from all the activity. This break in the action will prop up sagging spirits or create a relief valve to uncork building pressures.

Whatever you do, consider the needs of the total group. You could divide into subgroups—with an adult in each one—in order to meet the differing needs.

Let the group members relieve tension by sharing skits and silly songs. You'll relieve the group from the pressure of being on a serious mission with big responsibilities to the residents and each other. You'll give them permission to relax and play.

13. The end of the workcamp is a powerful experience. The power of helping other people and being the body of Christ for a neighbor pulls workcampers into worship on the closing night. Your challenge will be to channel the high emotions and energy from accomplishment into constructive celebration.

Many young people have never attended a camp that closed in a positive way. Often, undirected or misdirected energy is spent with shaving cream fights and draping toilet paper everywhere.

Workcamps grow out of a unique purpose and should be celebrated in special ways. Closing worship will celebrate all that has been good in the mission project. The group members can express sadness about the end of a week of wonderful works. They'll focus on success and release all the fear that "I might not measure up." This closing celebration will offer healing for inadequacies and insecurities. Young people will affirm their power to serve in the name of Jesus Christ.

Freedom to share will flow powerfully in this kind of worship. Form circles with the work crews and ask them to pass a lighted candle to each worker. Ask each worker to state one thing another person did for which the crew can be thankful. The worker passes the candle to the person, who repeats the process. Continue until every person has been affirmed.

Allow a time for the total group to relate the week's highlights. The group members will be looking once again at the times when they saw God working through the work crews and the residents.

Surprising stories may be told. Estelle was a spoiled seventh-grader who expected to be coddled wherever she was. After two days of getting nowhere in her attempts to be the princess of the workcamp, she suffered the ultimate indignity of being assigned to clean bathrooms in a very dirty home for the elderly. Immediately, the group crowned her the "Biffy Queen."

In her anger and out of pride, Estelle vowed to show the crew members the most sparkling bathrooms they had ever seen. By the end of the workcamp, her determination had built her into a real team player. She even fashioned a crown to wear on the final night to celebrate her new skill in cleaning bathrooms. She thanked the group for shocking her out of her spoiled habits and expectations. She prayed that she would be able to continue her growth as a servant rather than being someone who expected to be served.

Crews can share the experiences that occurred as they completed their projects—how it felt to say goodbye to their new friends; their sense of loss as they leave the community and begin to see what they've gained.

The group needs to focus its vision on a larger commitment to service and the process of making new friends in the days ahead. Making new friends naturally grows out of sharing God's love. The group members can begin looking ahead to creating ways of sharing God's love when they return home.

As a youth group, brainstorm for activities and plans to express God's love back home. These ideas can be personal actions within families or group actions within the church or community. List the ideas on a sheet of paper; ask each youth group member to sign it.

Gather the entire group in a circle and place the sheet of paper in the center. Offer personal prayers for the ministries still ahead. Prayers of thanksgiving and praise can fill the group with a spirit of celebration. You've completed a week of pouring out love in the name and power of Jesus Christ.

Challenge the group members to share their feelings of growth and acceptance they felt during the week.

Ask everyone to commit the final night of the workcamp to a process of building relationships, rather than messing up the place of lodging. Friendship can elevate the group to spend their last night with hugs and handshakes as expressions of love.

14. Leaving the workcamp includes certain responsibilities. Clean the work areas before the crews leave. Haul away all trash and residue from the work effort. You'll leave a blight on the community if you pile trash in some little old lady's yard and let her clean it up. If you plan ahead, your local contact person will be able to arrange for hauling away the debris.

Don't leave the cleanup for local people to do after the workcamp. The best time to clean up is the last workday. Young people like to see their project cleaned up and complete. They will carry a lasting impression of how the residence looked when they left it. If some crews must work late to finish, make arrangements to finish the cleanup process the next day.

Pack all tools and equipment, using your checklists to

ensure that you return with everything you brought and
no more. Impress on the work crews the need to clean all
tools thoroughly before packing them. Be particularly careful of the tools or equipment you may have from the local
agency. Maintain a good image by returning the tools you
used in clean and usable condition.

Clean the lodging and eating area. Your hosts will
remember you for what you left or didn't leave behind.
Your impression will be lasting and negative if you leave a
mess.

Settle your accounts with the local agency, vendors of
materials and other services. Again, you will give a bad impression if you leave with unpaid bills or without making
arrangements for payment. Some organizations need several days to prepare billing statements. Others can't sur-
vive if you don't pay. Always check about payments.

Talk with the local contact person about people you
will need to see before you leave. Be deliberate and careful about your departure. If you look too eager to leave,
people will grow suspicious and wonder why you are
hurrying.

Whenever final goodbyes happen with the residents,
encourage everyone to exchange mailing addresses. It's
difficult to get an address after you leave the community.
It also looks like an afterthought if you ask for an address
several weeks after the workcamp.

Encourage the work crews to share prayers with the
residents. Crew members will know if the residents will be
open to share in prayer. Otherwise, offer prayer as a crew
and then say your goodbyes.

Departures demand prayers. Whether spoken or simply felt, prayers will soar from the spirits of the young
people through shining faces or tear-soaked eyes. You'll
know the intensity of the prayers by the feeling in the
kids' voices.

Speak your prayers for the whole group. Consecrate
the place and the efforts of the workcamp as a signal to all
the world that God is working through his people in a

Chart 17
Workcamp Evaluation Form

1. What did you like most about the workcamp?

2. What are your strongest feelings or reactions about the week?

3. What would you change?

4. What would you leave the same?

5. How would you rate the travel planning?

Good   10   9   8   7   6   5   4   3   2   1   Poor

Explain your rating:

6. What would you do differently with travel planning?

7. How would you rate your training and preparation for the workcamp?

Good   10   9   8   7   6   5   4   3   2   1   Poor

Explain your rating:

8. How would you rate the fund-raising projects?

Good   10   9   8   7   6   5   4   3   2   1   Poor

Explain your rating:

9. What do you suggest for the youth group as a result of the workcamp? (Please be specific: who, when, where, what would happen)

10. What other suggestions do you have?

Permission to photocopy this chart granted for local church use only. Copyright © 1987 by Group Books, Inc., Box 481, Loveland, CO 80539.

special way.

15. Evaluate the workcamp experience. Evaluation of the workcamp experience will be the backbone for your plans for the coming year. Have the group members write out their impressions of the workcamp. You can use copies of Chart 17, which is a sample evaluation form. Revise it as necessary to meet your needs for specific program evaluation.

Ideas from the evaluations can be stirred into your regular program through discreet planning. Look for creative ways to use the new strengths of the kids, while being realistic about the effort you can expect from them over the next year.

You now have at least one advantage as you approach the coming year—you have experienced planners and organizers to help with the next activities and projects. They have seen what can happen when a group organizes and carefully prepares to get a job done. They know the group can work together and accomplish exciting results. And they know one person should not do all the work.

Chapter Ten
The Trip Home

One of the biggest services you can offer young people is the opportunity to talk about whatever is important to them at the present moment. If you stay at home for your workcamp, schedule a day for these important debriefing processes. If you travel to a workcamp, the trip home is a unique opportunity to discuss kids' feelings about the workcamp. The immediacy of the sharing helps the kids remember all they can. You'll stimulate much better recall than if you wait until you get home to try to reminisce.

If you will be traveling for several days by bus, you can schedule morning or evening time for small group discussions. Or, you can plan for discussions en route if you're riding in vans or cars, since kids will already be in groups.

Approach the process as a game by encouraging kids to remember everything possible, not just the highlights. Memories shared by one person may trigger someone else's. Group sharing will enable kids to recall more than they might on their own. This instant-replay type of discussion maximizes kids' memories and experiences. Workcampers build a layer of understanding by recalling what happened and then talking about those experiences.

Discussions on the trip home also serve as resources for discussions during the following months. Throughout the year, group members will form values out of their workcamp experiences. They'll need to sort out the various levels of importance contained in each experience they remember.

Facilitate talk time while traveling by following these

guidelines:

1. Encourage each person to describe the times that are bombarding his or her memory. By carefully describing workcamp memories, kids will experience many of the same feelings that bubbled up during the event. You can recognize each person's most important memories by noting the intensity in which he or she describes them. At first, discussions may center on safe, fun topics. However, over a period of days the group members will share deeper feelings and their most important times.

2. Relate the group's experiences to the scriptures studied during the workcamp. Remind the young people that the scriptures connect with their efforts to give to others. Scriptures clarify the meaning of servanthood.

Ask kids to think about Jesus' example of servanthood when he washed the disciples' feet. Then, ask kids to travel back in their memories through each day of the workcamp. What are examples of servanthood kids saw in other members of their crew? in the residents? in the agency helpers?

3. Discuss puzzling experiences. Sometimes events that don't make much sense at first mean more after careful examination.

One workcamp crew finished its project early, then was assigned to clean out an old cemetery. From the start of the day, Rob complained that the crew was assigned a rotten job. He made bad jokes about working in a graveyard. The group struggled to figure out why he reacted as he did, since he usually did anything asked of him without a murmur. Uncharacteristic behavior clued them in to the deeper feelings Rob was experiencing in relation to death.

After some discussion, Rob blurted out that the cemetery had made him remember the death of his grandfather. They had been very close, and when the grandfather died suddenly, Rob had tried to "be strong" and not break down in tears. His powerful feelings about the loss of his grandfather created unusual reactions about the graveyard.

As the group members listened to Rob, they began to relate their feelings about death. They discussed the resources of faith that Christians could use when faced with loss and feelings of grief. At the end of the talk, Rob confided that he had told the group more about how much he missed his "Paw Paw" than he had been able to tell his parents. He admitted that he felt much better after talking about his grandfather.

Discussing memories, especially the difficult ones, leads to a clearer awareness of God's will. It's not hard to imagine that God may have wanted the group to work in a cemetery so Rob could lead the group to a better understanding of God's loving care at a time of sorrow. Many opportunities fall into the dark recesses of our minds, just because we do not examine what we have experienced more closely.

4. Build kids' confidence by affirming their accomplishments. New skills and personal resources are fun to develop and are helpful in other areas of life. For example, workcamps may develop skills in resolving conflict. Those same skills may help at home when family problems erupt.

The ability to cope with new situations builds confidence. Many young people fear going to new events because they are not sure they can handle the unknown experiences. After kids participate in a workcamp and deal with the many unknowns, they feel confident they can handle other new challenges such as going to college or beginning their first full-time job.

Adults can reaffirm the abilities of young people by helping them process their experiences at a workcamp and helping them affirm their individual strengths. Kids can build confidence for the future and face it as people with strength and ability.

Workcampers can look for other ways to use their new-found skills and confidence. They may decide to plan a workcamp in their town. They may decide to set aside one workday each month to repair needy people's homes, or to run errands for them. Young people who have captured the vision of Christian service will launch out as powerful servants in the church.

5. Discuss how you will share with others the excitement about the workcamp. Heading toward home raises the question about young people who didn't participate in the trip and new kids who may wish to join the group. Plan to share fully but tactfully the excitement of the trip. The workcamp experience can be presented as a gift offered to those who couldn't attend. That gift may be accepted or rejected.

Some young people may hear about the new experiences and feel cheated by not going on the trip. If this happens, listen to their reactions. Try to build a bridge between those who went and those who stayed. Remember that the initial reaction may not be the final reaction.

Other people who didn't attend a workcamp may feel guilty for not "doing their part" with the group, even if they had no choice but to stay home. Working to accept all members fully, regardless of their missing the workcamp, is an important goal for each workcamper.

6. Make plans to involve non-participants in future projects. This direct effort to include others who didn't participate in the workcamp will relieve their worries about being left out of the group's future work projects. Brainstorm for general ideas on the trip home. Talk about some of the ideas kids thought of at the workcamp. Once you return home, you can plan the details of the projects.

Workcampers can teach the non-participants skills they learned at the camp: painting, rescreening, building steps, etc. This training time builds community and helps all kids feel a part of the group. Encourage the workcampers to affirm and praise others in the skills they are developing.

7. Consciously plan to stop looking back and to start looking ahead. Plan a definite time frame in which to complete your reporting. After the reporting period is finished, focus on new activities and projects. This approach will limit the overkill of workcamp memories.

Workcampers can help one another maintain some vigilance about overworking the stories they have brought home. When reminiscing has gone too far, someone needs to signal to the others to change the subject.

The group members can look actively for new things to talk about after the workcamp has been rehashed enough. They should consciously decide to move on to new topics.

Talking about the concerns of returning home will help everyone become aware of the issues involved in re-entry. Group members will develop more sensitivity toward friends and families who may grow weary of work-camp stories. They will know when the old stories are dragged into too many conversations too many times.

The trip home can carve a time of growth out of the reactions to the workcamp. Young people will enjoy the process of making plans as a result of their experience. But they naturally will want to move on to new adventures, particularly because the workcamp has meant so much to them. Use the travel time to its fullest, since it may be the last time you have to grow with this extraordinary group of people.

Chapter Eleven

Re-Entry Into the Everyday World

When your group returns home, will Christian service flow from the young people as it did at the workcamp? Or will the energizing experiences of the workcamp fade into memory to become only shadows of the realities you've created?

Groups without a plan and purpose lose much of what they have gained and learned. To avoid deteriorating in spirit like the crumbling houses they have seen, the group members need to channel their attention into new activities during the coming months.

Explore and discover ways to become a new group at home. The workcampers have created a dynamic self-image during their week of serving. Now they must re-create that reality for friends, family, church and community. Otherwise, the young people will be deceiving everyone at home about who they have become.

Pray that the group members receive insight to understand the possibilities God gives them. Awareness of God's will can flow from your group at home as well as at the workcamp. Plunge into that awareness by reading and discussing the scriptures that were helpful during the workcamp. Look at the scriptures from the perspective of how they apply to your home community. What are the new directions you can take as a group because of your new identity as servants of Christ? Have any possibilities been overlooked in the past, simply because you did not know the power you possessed as servants?

Group members have experienced God within their lives through the reality of his love. The self-giving efforts made possible by the workcamp can now be repeated in new ways. Planning service opportunities helps kids love their neighbors as they love themselves.

Ask the young people to describe times when they felt God most completely during the workcamp. List the activities that were occurring during these times. Did the special feelings come during group discussions? times of conflict? the completion of a day of work? the end of the project when residents expressed appreciation? worship when members opened themselves to God?

From this list of significant times, brainstorm without censorship or reservation possibilities for projects and activities. Develop the ideas for service the kids thought of at the workcamp and on the trip home. List all possible activities your group could handle during the next six months. What can your group do in your home community or nearby to continue to serve? How can the workcamp experiences and activities once again sprout through the soil in the backyard of your church? community? homes? What can you do to create similar circumstances and opportunities?

Look at your community with fresh eyes. Where can you channel the power you discovered at the workcamp into specific projects of volunteer service? You may uncover possibilities you never knew existed, just by talking with people who work with elderly and low-income people. Learn of needy people by visiting nurses associations or services, social welfare programs, community action programs, ministerial associations and United Way administrators. Chart 18 lists ideas for servanthood projects you could plan.

One youth group started doing community service projects after a GROUP Workcamp and has engaged in lo-

Chart 18
Servanthood Projects

1. Paint and weatherize elderly church members' homes.
2. Offer a special babysitting service for handicapped or seriously ill children.
3. Volunteer to coach disabled athletes or to sponsor a Special Olympic event of your own.
4. Visit shut-ins and those who are sick and hospitalized.
5. Sponsor a local mini-workcamp.
6. Plan a canned food distribution service on a regular basis for needy people in your community.
7. Read for blind individuals. Record stories on cassettes.
8. Sponsor an errand-running service. Pick up and deliver prescriptions or grocery shop for someone.
9. Mow lawns, do general yardwork in the summer and shovel walks in the winter for the elderly.
10. Visit nursing homes. Plan special programs such as clown and puppet ministry.
11. Plan barbecues and special dinners at orphanages, foster-care facilities and halfway houses.
12. Sponsor "Mother's morning out" by organizing a summer babysitting service one morning a week at the church.
13. Help with Bible school, Sunday school and nursery school.
14. Organize a senior citizens banquet, complete with food and a program.
15. Participate in a woodcutting project for needy people in the area.
16. Help with community cleanup projects.
17. Volunteer for office work at community-service organizations.
18. Volunteer to help at the hospital.
19. Raise funds to replenish books and magazines for hospitals.
20. Donate flowers from your Sunday service to sick, lonely people in the hospital.
21. Help with church spring-cleaning. Do yardwork, wash windows, etc. Donate to charities the funds the church would have used.
22. Volunteer to work at libraries and museums. Sponsor tours for the elderly and for children during the summer.
23. Sponsor children's outings to skating rinks, state parks, amusement parks and pools.
24. Organize fund raisers and donate the earned money to local or national charities.
25. Sponsor Christmas parties for special groups such as the elderly or handicapped. (Provide punch, cookies and singing.)
26. Organize a New Year's Eve babysitting service at the church.
27. Sponsor a refugee family or child.
28. Cook for Ronald McDonald houses or similar institutions—especially around holidays.
29. Work with crisis hot lines.
30. Provide transportation to services for church members who can't drive.
31. Join a Big Brother/Big Sister program.
32. Gather used clothes for inner-city missions.
33. Collect and recycle aluminum cans and newspapers. Donate proceeds to the poor.

cal projects ever since. Rick, a volunteer youth worker
from South Carolina, explored possibilities with his group
and then they set up a weekend workcamp in their city.
The follow-up workcamp not only involved new people,
but it got them interested in preparing for a big summer
workcamp the following year. It created a simple way to
involve new people in the group. And it pulled back into
the group the folks who didn't get to go to the summer
event.

Experienced workcampers trained new workers in carpentry skills. Then new people could better relate to the
group and no longer felt left out. Rick's group continued
to grow through various forms of workcamping over many
years. And those who experienced workcamping have
grown to deeper levels of commitment.

You can schedule work projects throughout the year
such as repairing family dwellings, helping older people,
refurbishing struggling churches and working on community facilities.

Relationship skills practiced at the workcamp provide
an exciting resource for serving in the church. Young people can visit with shut-ins and residents of rest homes, and
possibly assist with community programs for preschool or
day care. A potent ability to listen and communicate in a
caring way will help young people in any setting.

After you've completed a list of project ideas for the
next six months, ask the kids to brainstorm for ways to
encourage new people to take part in all that you plan.
How can you welcome more young people into the group
and prevent their feeling like outsiders? Since other people
will sense a special feeling among those who attended the
workcamp, only a conscious effort will bring new people
into the group.

Plan to incorporate new people into the group's work,
moving beyond the concern about not sharing a past experience. Those who experienced the workcamp will need
to learn to enjoy the inner satisfaction of having experienced the workcamp without always talking about it.

As previously mentioned, train kids who didn't participate in a workcamp, then invite them to help in future work projects.

Affirm all kids by making care cards a regular part of your youth program, not simply an affirmation activity done at the workcamp. Give the group members each a Manila envelope and a marker. Have them write their names on the front and decorate them. Hang the care card envelopes on a wall or bulletin board. Always keep a supply of 3×5 cards and pencils nearby. Throughout the year, ask kids to write affirmation notes and place them in corresponding envelopes. Use care cards during special times of the year or for special projects. Some groups use care cards once per month as a way of affirming each other.

Continue affirmation exercises throughout the year as the kids grow and change, and as new people become a regular part of the group. Young people need affirmation regularly, so any way you can offer that kind of experience will help build a positive self-image. You also will be reinforcing their self-value over a period of time as you provide opportunities for them to be servants.

Chapter Twelve
The Report to the Church

The workcamp gave you all the ingredients for a top-quality report to your church. All you need to do is organize them into a snappy, exciting, accurate, emotionally and spiritually powerful presentation that represents the growth and experiences at the workcamp. A report can be fun, but don't make it too long. Choose what you will report to the congregation and what you will leave for informal sharing times. Here's how to prepare your report:

1. Review the evaluations from the group. These comments will tell you what activities were most important to the young people. Remember those powerful points and decide how to highlight them in your presentation. Your youth group plans for the coming months will grow out of those evaluation results, making them the visible outcome of the workcamp experience.

2. Synchronize quality slides and taped interviews. Through the powerful impact of a slide show and taped interviews, you can describe what happened throughout the workcamp experience.

Give the congregation an initial picture of what workcamping is about by starting the slide show with scenes of workers and projects. Write a script for the show's narration. Include all the preparatory phases that started months before the camp, and work your way through the process that made the workcamp possible. By writing a narrative, you can control the length of the show. If you don't want to use narration, show the slides chronologically to tell the story visually in a way that will not confuse anyone.

Include as many shots as possible of the church members involved in the fund-raising projects and other preparations. Let the story grow through the support of many people from the church and the community. The young people are the stars, but church members are the supporting cast.

Slides showing travel experiences to and from the site will tell the story of the variety of challenges the youth group experienced. Limit the recreational shots, since side trips were not the main purpose of the workcamp.

Workcamps can squeal with fun. Show the church how workcampers balanced work and play, even though the majority of the time was invested in hard work. Parents will want to know the trip was not all drudgery.

Show pictures of workers applying their skills on the project. Use as many of these shots as you can, and be sure at least one slide presents each workcamper. No one likes to be left out. Just remember not to allow the show to get too long. Mix up the shots so there are groups working, individuals working, fun shots and serious shots. Lots of work shots will tell the story of service.

Give the congregation a feel for the friendship that developed during the project by including several slides of residents, agency supervisors and other community leaders interacting with the workcampers. Play the taped interviews with people while you show the corresponding slides.

Show the meaningful fellowship that took place at mealtimes. Enhance the image of the trip by capturing some of the personal interaction that took place during sack-lunch discussions, early morning breakfasts and evening campfires.

Many workcamps feature special activities in the evening to promote growth and inspiration. Show the congregation some of the ways you celebrated your time of service. They'll be amazed that people who worked so hard with big projects during the day also could have so much activity and fun in the evenings.

Portray the cultural presentations you enjoyed in the evenings. Cultural understanding is one of the purposes of going to another area to do workcamps. After the slide show, let kids explain more about the cultural exchange.

Before-and-after shots of the work projects tell the story of significant work that was accomplished. Many homes will show an impressive change in appearance over the course of a week. Picture the crew members who worked on the home and some of the individual jobs they accomplished. Before-and-after shots are great ways to show the drastic results of the refurbishing.

Save some poignant pictures for the closing of the slide show. Picture residents and workcampers saying goodbyes and expressing their feelings with smiles and hugs.

3. Tell the complete story of the workcamp. Ask members of the group to give brief descriptions of specific, significant experiences. Select stories so that each person relates something different about the workcamp. Each person's closing remarks can indicate the difference the workcamp experience made in his or her life. Have the kids each write out their description and read it so it can be timed. Coordinate these individual reports so they last no longer than three minutes each. Caution each person to stick to the planned comments and descriptions they have written. Otherwise, the report could go on for hours.

Ask a few kids to describe the residents' reactions to the group and the emotional or spiritual impact the workcamp experience made in the residents' lives. Specific comments or descriptions of residents' reactions will personalize the report and its effect on local people.

If kids recorded their feelings in journals, invite them to read short excerpts to capture an eyewitness account of what happened at certain times.

4. Present a token of your thanks. Thank the church members for their support by giving them mementos from the workcamp. Present appropriate mementos such as artifacts, small rugs and cultural symbols.

5. Read special scriptures. Clarify once again the value and importance of serving others. Select a few scriptures about servanthood that best fit your group's experience. (Use the scriptures discussed on your trip home. Which verses meant the most to the kids? See the listing of servanthood scriptures in the Appendix for more ideas.) Read them to the congregation as the guiding reasons for what you have done and expect to do in the future.

6. Present the list of planned projects for the upcoming year. Ask group members to report on the projects they want to do for the next year that reflect the workcamp experiences. Have them describe how the workcamp contributed to the youth program and resulted in other projects.

Highlight the skills, insights and spiritual growth that now are present in the youth group, and consecrate them to the continuing mission of the church. Present the list of planned projects as a symbol of the kids' dedication to servanthood.

Communicate your hope for the further growth of the young people so their faith and service will shine as beacons to the world. Ask church members to pray for the youth group's ongoing mission as personal servants of God.

Epilogue

Workcamp participants usually come home beaming with self-esteem and self-confidence. Workcamps produce the raw material that pushes teenagers to discover their potential. They begin to perform services that make a difference. They learn to drive a tractor, operate a power tool, cook for a crowd, use first-aid training, milk a cow, build a fence, insulate a wall, glaze a window, paint a porch or tell a story. After succeeding at a workcamp, kids' confidence level grows. And they feel wonderful!

Adult advisers experience the same consequences. The power of serving in the name and spirit of Jesus Christ propels them into feelings of value and meaning. In addition, adults experience the growth and immediate reactions of the young people in their group. After a workcamp, adult sponsors are filled with a special warmth that radiates through their faith commitment.

The unpredictable power of workcamps reaches into many unexpected corners of life. Almost as if by accident, the blessings of workcamping spread to families who had no idea they were engaging in something special.

Mary and Tom came to church and youth group because a friend invited them. Their parents showed no interest in the church, but they grudgingly allowed their children to participate. The group was surprised when the two were allowed to attend the workcamp.

As the days passed at the workcamp, Mary and Tom became more and more lively. They served as "spark plugs" for the whole group. On the last night, these two teenagers brought everyone to tears as they described how the love and care of the workcamp community had energized their lives. They felt a special purpose in the youth group that they hadn't experienced before.

Those days of intentional Christian community deeply affected the lives of Mary and Tom. The other 18 work-campers also discovered their power to make a difference in the lives of others. This power can't be ignored in a workcamp community.

No one can predict the surprises that will happen in the fluid environment of a workcamp. Demands and opportunities change every minute, because so many different people are involved.

In spite of the unforeseen, any group can plan and carry out a workcamp. Careful, detailed organization of each step builds the foundation for effective youth group service projects. Anticipating possible problems and planning possible solutions in advance prepares you for whatever happens. Then you can manage a workcamp with all its surprises.

But surprises can be fun and induce growth. One group carried buckets of water up two flights of stairs in order to flush broken toilets. Another group of workcampers slept in a barn for the first time in their lives. Nearly everyone has slept in the same room with adult advisers who snored. Others tasted goat's milk or ate mutton for the first time. Some saw sheep slaughtered and witnessed the stewardship of using every part of an animal for something necessary. Some felt the sting of wasps or ants or chiggers or monstrous mosquitos. One little guy was showered with surprise when his pastor got sick suddenly and upchucked all over him.

Other surprises carry more meaning. Shy and hesitant young people have discovered they can speak before a large audience when they have reported exciting events at their work site. Overwhelming applause at a talent show has catapulted some young people into efforts to develop their natural abilities. Adults who had been discouraged by a plodding youth program and indifference from the young people have been shocked by the excitement of those same young people who discovered servant ministries. God uses surprises to generate new life in his people.

Some young people even create surprises for a workcamp. Benny and Jeff felt tremendous appreciation for their experience at a workcamp early in the summer. They were bursting with a need to do more, but their workcamp was finished. Knowing that other workcamps were performing their special form of magic, Benny and Jeff reacted creatively. They volunteered to help behind the scenes at another workcamp.

They showed up almost salivating at the prospect of working on the staff. They volunteered for every extra job that appeared. Their enthusiasm bolstered the staff's sagging spirits from long hours of hard work. At the end of the week, Benny and Jeff bounced into their car, grinned and waved goodbye with a new workcamp experience lodged in their memory banks. The staff wished it had a Benny and Jeff at every workcamp.

Talents and abilities blossom as young people reach out cautiously, faithfully and uncertainly. But their new awareness of the power of love tells them they are not alone. They know God is working with his servants. They have felt God's presence in a swarming bunch of workers who call on the name of his Son and follow him whenever there is need.

The power of workcamps springs from the love of God, who launches us into the paths of service because his love lives in us.

We need no other reason.

Appendix

A. Servanthood Scriptures (NIV)

Matthew 5:41-42: "If someone forces you to go one mile, go with him two miles. Give to the one who asks you, and do not turn away from the one who wants to borrow from you."

Matthew 7:16-20: "By their fruit you will recognize them. Do people pick grapes from thornbushes, or figs from thistles? Likewise every good tree bears good fruit, but a bad tree bears bad fruit. A good tree cannot bear bad fruit, and a bad tree cannot bear good fruit. Every tree that does not bear good fruit is cut down and thrown into the fire. Thus, by their fruit you will recognize them."

Matthew 13:31-32: He told them another parable: "The kingdom of heaven is like a mustard seed, which a man took and planted in his field. Though it is the smallest of all your seeds, yet when it grows, it is the largest of garden plants and becomes a tree, so that the birds of the air come and perch in its branches."

Matthew 22:39: "And the second is like it: 'Love your neighbor as yourself.' "

Matthew 25:40: "The King will reply, 'I tell you the truth, whatever you did for one of the least of these brothers of mine, you did for me.' "

Mark 8:34: Then he called the crowd to him along with his disciples and said: "If anyone would come after me, he must deny himself and take up his cross and follow me."

Mark 10:43-45: "Not so with you. Instead, whoever wants to become great among you must be your servant, and whoever wants to be first must be slave of all. For even the Son of Man did not come to be served, but to serve, and to give his life as a ransom for many."

Luke 6:32-36: "If you love those who love you, what credit is that to you? Even 'sinners' love those who love them. And if you do good to those who are good to you, what credit is that to you? Even 'sinners' do that. And if you lend to those from whom you expect repayment, what credit is that to you? Even 'sinners' lend to 'sinners,' expecting to be repaid in full. But love your enemies, do good to them, and lend to them without expecting to get anything back. Then your reward will be great, and you will be sons of the Most High, because he is kind to the ungrateful and wicked. Be merciful, just as your Father is merciful."

Luke 6:37: "Do not judge, and you will not be judged. Do not condemn, and you will not be condemned. Forgive, and you will be forgiven."

Luke 10:29-37: But he wanted to justify himself, so he asked Jesus,

"And who is my neighbor?"

In reply Jesus said: "A man was going down from Jerusalem to Jericho, when he fell into the hands of robbers. They stripped him of his clothes, beat him and went away, leaving him half dead. A priest happened to be going down the same road, and when he saw the man, he passed by on the other side. So too, a Levite, when he came to the place and saw him, passed by on the other side. But a Samaritan, as he traveled, came where the man was; and when he saw him, he took pity on him. He went to him and bandaged his wounds, pouring on oil and wine. Then he put the man on his own donkey, took him to an inn and took care of him. The next day he took out two silver coins and gave them to the innkeeper. 'Look after him,' he said, 'and when I return, I will reimburse you for any extra expense you may have.'

"Which of these three do you think was a neighbor to the man who fell into the hands of robbers?"

The expert in the law replied, "The one who had mercy on him."

Jesus told him, "Go and do likewise."

Luke 14:28-30: "Suppose one of you wants to build a tower. Will he not first sit down and estimate the cost to see if he has enough money to complete it? For if he lays the foundation and is not able to finish it, everyone who sees it will ridicule him, saying, 'This fellow began to build and was not able to finish.' "

John 12:26: "Whoever serves me must follow me; and where I am, my servant also will be. My Father will honor the one who serves me."

John 21:15-17: When they had finished eating, Jesus said to Simon Peter, "Simon son of John, do you truly love me more than these?"

"Yes, Lord," he said, "you know that I love you."

Jesus said, "Feed my lambs."

Again Jesus said, "Simon son of John, do you truly love me?"

He answered, "Yes, Lord, you know that I love you."

Jesus said, "Take care of my sheep."

The third time he said to him, "Simon son of John, do you love me?"

Peter was hurt because Jesus asked him the third time, "Do you love me?" He said, "Lord, you know all things; you know that I love you."

Jesus said, "Feed my sheep."

Romans 13:8-10: Let no debt remain outstanding, except the continuing debt to love one another, for he who loves his fellow man has fulfilled the law. The commandments, "Do not commit adultery," "Do not murder," "Do not steal," "Do not covet," and whatever other commandment there may be, are summed up in this one rule: "Love your neighbor as yourself." Love does no harm to its neighbor. Therefore love is the fulfillment of the law.

Romans 15:1-2: We who are strong ought to bear with the failings of the weak and not to please ourselves. Each of us should please his neighbor for his good, to build him up.

Galatians 5:22-23: But the fruit of the Spirit is love, joy, peace, patience, kindness, goodness, faithfulness, gentleness and self-control. Against such things there is no law.

Galatians 6:9-10: Let us not become weary in doing good, for at the proper time we will reap a harvest if we do not give up. Therefore, as we have opportunity, let us do good to all people, especially to those who belong to the family of believers.

Ephesians 2:10: For we are God's workmanship, created in Christ Jesus to do good works, which God prepared in advance for us to do.

2 Timothy 1:7: For God did not give us a spirit of timidity, but a spirit of power, of love and of self-discipline.

Hebrews 13:1-2: Keep on loving each other as brothers. Do not forget to entertain strangers, for by so doing some people have entertained angels without knowing it.

James 1:22: Do not merely listen to the word, and so deceive yourselves. Do what it says.

James 2:14-18: What good is it, my brothers, if a man claims to have faith but has no deeds? Can such faith save him? Suppose a brother or sister is without clothes and daily food. If one of you says to him, "Go, I wish you well; keep warm and well fed," but does nothing about his physical needs, what good is it? In the same way, faith by itself, if it is not accompanied by action, is dead.

But someone will say, "You have faith; I have deeds." Show me your faith without deeds, and I will show you my faith by what I do.

1 John 3:17-18: If anyone has material possessions and sees his brother in need but has no pity on him, how can the love of God be in him? Dear children, let us not love with words or tongue but with actions and in truth.

1 John 4:12: No one has ever seen God; but if we love each other, God lives in us and his love is made complete in us.

1 John 4:20-21: If anyone says, "I love God," yet hates his brother, he is a liar. For anyone who does not love his brother, whom he has seen, cannot love God, whom he has not seen. And he has given us this command: Whoever loves God must also love his brother.

B. Role Plays

Use these role plays to help your group members prepare for the workcamp. (Chapter 7 includes instructions on how to lead role plays.) Process the role plays by praising appropriate actions and statements. Have the group look for ways to improve the actions and statements. Point out how specific behaviors can create problems or misunderstandings. Look for careful communication (see Appendix C for information on basic communication skills).

A Dictator in the Crew

● *Setting:* Your crew has been working together for two days now. It's not as fun as you thought it would be. That's because one person in your group operates like an Army sergeant. He bosses everybody around and doesn't allow anyone else to make decisions. Instead of feeling good about the work, you're beginning to resent it.

● *Guidelines:* Have one person be the dictator who tells everybody what to do. Have two crew members initiate a confrontation with the dictator. Assign one crew member to side with the dictator. Have the others cooperate in helping to change the situation and express their feelings.

● *Questions:* Should you try to change someone who's bothering you? Why or why not? How can you approach the problem without hurting someone? How can you approach the problem if you feel intimidated or scared? What actions or responses would lead to effectively handling the situation? If things don't get better, what should you try to do? What would Jesus do?

Is There a Reasonable Compromise?

● *Setting:* The homeowner is a lonely widow. She desperately wants to talk every minute of the day. Her insistence on talking has lured two guys and one girl into sitting down with her in the kitchen for continuous conversations during the first two days. As a result, they haven't been any help and the crew's project is obviously not going to be completed without everyone working each day for the rest of the week.

● *Guidelines:* Assign someone to play the homeowner who continues to try to get people to talk. She can even suggest that she doesn't care if the work gets done.

One worker can be a realist: "The local agency has committed materials to this project and it must be completed."

Another worker can be a philosopher: "What if everyone stopped to talk? What if the whole workcamp didn't complete the work projects? Are we here just to talk? If we don't stop and listen, will our work be in vain?"

Another worker can be a mediator: "Can we work and talk? Can the lady help work?"

The talkers can defend the need to help relieve loneliness, then gradually explore ways to get the job done.

● *Questions:* Is it necessary to complete the work projects? Why or why not? How much visiting with residents is appropriate? What skills and personal strengths are needed to resolve conflicts when both sides have acceptable reasons for their positions?

Other Role Plays

● A local person offers some home-cooked food to the work crew.
● An orphan wants someone to adopt him.
● A local church fellowship wants your crew to return in the evening for a church meeting.

C. Building Better Communication

Review the descriptions of the following basic communication skills.

"I" Messages

Messages using "I" don't sound bossy. Say, "I would like some help with this plywood." Don't say, "Give me some help with the plywood." After a long day or tiring week, people may be sensitive and irritable. They may feel "bossed around," even when you don't mean to be bossy. Practice "I" messages with questions, requests and information. Make personal requests, not demands on others.

Write an "I" message for the next two questions:

1. How would you ask for help to set the table for a meal at the workcamp?

2. How would you tell a person he or she is bothering you by not helping?

"Feedback" Listening

Feedback listening is repeating what you hear. This way, the sender of the message has a chance to clarify the meaning. Follow these steps:

1. State in your own words what you think the other person said. Pay attention to:
   ● Content of message;
   ● Feelings expressed in the message; and
   ● Time and place the message was stated.
2. If you don't understand the message, ask the sender to restate it.
3. Repeat the message in your own words.
4. Repeat this process until the message is clearly understood.

This process demands accurate listening. It'll save time and hard feelings by making sure that misunderstandings don't take place.

Practice "I" messages and feedback listening in small groups. Use a situation in which the group must decide something together. Try these situations:
   ● Decide when to break for lunch.
   ● Talk out a problem such as a practical joke that disrupts the work of the crew.
   ● Handle a disagreement in which half the group wants to change jobs the next day, and half the group doesn't.
   ● Use your imagination to think of other situations.

Basic Problem-Solving Skills

Use "I" messages and feedback listening to solve problems. Follow these steps:

1. State the problem clearly.
2. Describe feelings and obstacles caused by the problem.
3. Brainstorm for solutions (exhaust possibilities).
4. Decide which possible solution to try first.
5. After a test period, decide how the chosen solution is working.

Practice these methods of problem-solving by role playing situa-

tions that could happen during the workcamp trip:
- One person in your work crew is doing a sloppy job of painting.
- A couple often slip off together rather than working.
- A crew member always criticizes others' work.
- An adult is making all the decisions (not letting the crew decide).

The goal of these role plays is to talk honestly with each other to solve a problem. Communicate to others that you are focusing on behavior and not on them. Certain *behaviors* may be unacceptable, but a *person* is always acceptable. Accepting one another produces mutually acceptable behavior. Accurate communication is essential for effective workcamp experiences.

Permission to photocopy this handout granted for local church use only.
Copyright © 1987 by Group Books, Inc., Box 481, Loveland, CO 80539.

D. Program Ideas

The following program ideas are for Sunday through Friday evenings. You can add other ideas such as more Bible verses, more discussion questions, movies, slide shows, cultural entertainment and so on. Be sure you include a time each night for crew members to tell the entire group about meaningful events that happened during the day. Close each evening with a prayer asking for God's continued guidance, support and love.

Sunday
Divide the group into two equal-numbered circles, one inside the other. Play some music and instruct the outside circle to move clockwise, and the inside circle to move counterclockwise. Stop the music. The people standing opposite each other are partners. Have them share their name, their year in school and "the weirdest thing that ever happened to you."

Continue in this same manner so the kids get to talk to several people. The last time you do this "musical-questions" activity, tell the pairs to stay together and share goals and expectations for the week by answering these questions:

1. What was your main reason for deciding to help other people through a workcamp?

2. What would make you feel good about your efforts to help other people during the workcamp?

Divide into prearranged crews, assign crew numbers and go over any details and job duties for the upcoming week.

Monday
Prayer Partners
Ask all youth group members to roam the room looking for someone they'd like to know better. Say that when you yell "Stop!" mem-

bers should each grab another person and share their favorite youth group memory. Do this three times. The fourth time, the person kids grab is their prayer partner for the week. Pass out 3×5 cards and pencils and have them write their name and a prayer concern. Partners keep these concerns and pray for each other throughout the week.

Discussion

Stay with prayer partners and discuss these questions:

1. What was the most exciting thing that happened on your way to the workcamp?

2. Which tool best describes you? (hammer, tape measure, sandpaper, saw, paint roller, pliers, shovel, etc.)

3. Tell a neat thing about your youth group.

4. What did you feel when you first saw your work site?

5. Did your feelings change as time went on? Explain.

6. What is the biggest difference in your lifestyle compared to the residents'?

7. How do you feel about the residents you met?

8. What was today most like?
   a. Army boot camp
   b. Well-oiled machine
   c. Boy Scouts or Girl Scouts
   d. Octopus
   e. Time bomb
   f. Mismatched socks
   g. Dictatorship

9. Offer a silent prayer for residents and for members of your crew.

Tuesday

String Race

Have the kids sit in separate circles with their crews. Run a long piece of kite string around each crew and tie a knot so there is one continuous circle. Tie a ribbon in front of one person in each crew. This is the starting point. On the word "Go" each group moves the ribbon around the circle as fast as possible without breaking it. Yell "Stop" after 15 seconds. See how far each circle's ribbon has traveled. Try again to see if there is improvement. Make comments each time about coordination, teamwork, etc.

Discussion

Divide into pairs and have each pair read Philippians 2:5-7: "Your attitude should be the same as that of Christ Jesus: Who, being in very nature God, did not consider equality with God something to be grasped, but made himself nothing, taking the very nature of a servant, being made in human likeness."

Then have pairs discuss these questions:

1. Describe your best experience so far at your work site.

2. When did you feel most like a servant today?

3. When did you feel most served by someone else today?
4. How can you be a servant to others in your youth group?
5. What acts of servanthood have you seen in your youth group?
6. Describe a time when you felt frustrated today.
7. Describe a time when you felt happy today.

Wednesday

Since this is the middle of your workweek, let kids have the afternoon off. Do activities such as shopping, swimming, washing clothes and writing letters.

Plan a talent show for the evening. Let everybody who wants to participate perform for the group. Encourage skits, songs, piano playing, etc. Award prizes to all participants as a thanks for their courage to perform!

Thursday
The Puzzle Game

Ask the crews each to form a circle. Give each crew a box containing a complete, simple jigsaw puzzle with 30-50 pieces. Then say: "One of the most important things we learn as Christians at a workcamp is how to work together with others. Putting these puzzles together will be an exercise in how we work together.

"One person in each crew deals out the puzzle pieces to every member so that everyone has about the same number of pieces. Do that now.

"Now that everyone has a stack of puzzle pieces, here are the rules for putting the puzzle together.

"None of the crew may speak while putting the puzzle together. The puzzle must be assembled in silence.

"No one may take someone else's puzzle piece, even when you know where it should be placed. People on the crew must voluntarily give up a piece.

"As soon as you complete your puzzle, stand up as a crew and give yourself a standing ovation. Then, I'll bring you a discussion guide for your crew to share.

"Go as quickly as possible. Let's see which crew can finish first. Any questions? Go!"

Discussion

1. Each person shares, "The hardest thing about us putting the puzzle together in silence was . . . "

2. Did anyone talk? If yes, discuss when and why.

3. How well did the team work together? Did one or two people take charge on their own? Did the group silently choose a leader? Explain.

4. Did anyone just grab someone else's puzzle piece without permission? Explain.

5. In what ways is the exercise like the way we work together as a

team on our project during the day? In what ways do we work well together? How can we improve the ways we work together?

6. Read the following verse: "The body is a unit, though it is made up of many parts; and though all its parts are many, they form one body" (1 Corinthians 12:12).

7. Have each person share, "One way the crew acted like a unit this week was . . . "

8. Close with a short prayer.

Friday

Divide into crews. Give them 10 minutes to share their best memories of the past week. Ask these questions:

● How did your crew members feel God's Spirit working for and through them?

● What evidence did you see of God working? (For example, changing attitudes, extra energy, more cooperation, problems solved and so on.)

Read Mark 9:2-10 which tells about Jesus, Peter, James and John going to a high mountain where Jesus was transfigured. Have the crews discuss these questions:

● What were some "mountaintops" for you this week?

● How have you been transfigured or transformed (changed, made different) this week?

● How have you been helped by the residents and others?

● What will you take back to others?

Ask the crews to close in prayer by affirming their relationships and seeking God's guidance for opportunities to serve when they go home.

Give each crew a lighted candle. Say, "Hand the lighted candle to someone in your crew and say, 'You have made a difference because . . . ' Be sure each person receives the candle."

Bible Appetizers for at the Work Site

Crews can use the following ideas during the day for their devotions. Ideas are included for one week—Monday through Friday.

Monday Devotion

Read John 6:5-14 where Jesus fed the 5,000. Answer these questions:

1. Jesus saw people in need (hungry) and used the resources available to meet those needs. How is the workcamp similar to this act of service?

2. Jesus evidently added something special to the feeding process. How can Jesus' presence in a workcamp make a difference?

3. "Feeding" is a way of providing for strength, growth and re-energizing. What kinds of feeding are possible within your work crew? between your crew and residents of the area? between you and other workcampers?

Tuesday Devotion

Read Isaiah 49:6 which refers to a "light to the nations." Answer these questions:

1. How is the workcamp like being a "light to the nation"?

2. Will the light be seen by everyone, or will some people miss seeing it? What would be the natural response of the "light" if someone misses seeing it?

3. Name some service possibilities for after the workcamp.

4. How can we show God's light in the work crew?

5. What could the work crew do to help each person be a "light" to others during this week?

Wednesday Devotion

Read Luke 10:1-5 which tells about the great commissioning. Answer these questions:

1. Why does Jesus send his disciples out two by two instead of one by one?

2. Verse 4 says, "Do not take a purse or bag or sandals." What qualities should you bring to the workcamp and what should you leave behind?

3. How can your qualities complement the abilities of other crew members?

4. How can a work crew bring "peace" to a house?

Thursday Devotion

Read 1 Corinthians 12:4-6 which tells about the variety of gifts; then read 1 Corinthians 12:14-21 describing how the body is made up of many parts. Answer these questions:

1. What is the value or purpose of each person having different gifts or skills?

2. How can your work crew support and show appreciation for each person's gifts and skills?

3. What can prevent cooperation or harmony within the body?

4. What do you think God intends to have "the body" do to be most effective?

5. Will the individuals gain more or lose more by relying on each other for various skills and functions? Explain.

Friday Devotion

Read 1 Corinthians 13:8-13 which tells about love never ending. Answer these questions:

1. Now that the week is drawing to a close, share some of the growth you have experienced through the workcamp.

2. Tell your crew members the ways in which you have seen them grow through the workcamp experience.

3. Talk about ways in which you can ensure that your love for your resident and your crew members will continue and grow.

E. Fund Raisers

To help you make a successful trip, here is a collection of proven fund-raising ideas. These are new and old winners that have earned other groups like yours large amounts of money. With careful planning and dedication, your group can raise money in a short time.

1. Mission Luncheons—A good way to publicize and raise funds for a youth trip is to sponsor "Mission Luncheons." After Sunday worship services, many people eat out, so why not serve a hot lunch in the church at a reasonable price?

The members of one youth group served lunch four Sundays in May after church services. Parents were recruited to help. They prepared food such as barbecue chicken, slaw and salad, corn on the cob, hot rolls, tea, coffee and dessert. Children's portions cost less. They had carryout dishes available in snap-close Styrofoam containers. They publicized the lunches and encouraged the congregation to support their effort.

2. Windshield-Wiper Brigade—A group of Texas high school students raised funds for a local mission project with a "Windshield-Wiper Brigade."

Enthusiastic students, armed with clean rags and window cleaner, worked one Saturday afternoon at the parking lot of a large shopping mall. They placed colorful posters at the entrance of the parking lot which told of the fund raiser. The posters said: "Help us find our way to the mission site. Let us clean your windshields."

Offering to clean car windows for a 25-cent donation, they found a surprising response from shoppers. The cleaning process took an average of one minute, and generous tips were offered to the workers to clean the chrome or dashboard. They had a steady clientele with shoppers arriving in large numbers throughout the day.

With the decline and expense of full-service gas stations, shoppers were pleased at this low-cost convenience provided by the students.

At the end of an extremely busy day, the group members found they had earned twice as much money as anticipated and made plans to work at other large parking lots across the city for future projects.

With little preparation and a small investment in spray window cleaners, this innovative idea turned into a profitable success.

3. Buy a Mile—This project is a takeoff on the old "rising thermometer" idea.

Members of a youth group in Oregon took a large colored sheet of posterboard and sketched a map of their travel route to and from the workcamp. They added travel expenses and divided by the total number of miles they'd travel. Using this cost-per-mile estimate, they drew a red line over their route to show how far they'd get on the money received thus far.

Church members were given the opportunity over the next few months to help advance the kids around the route by buying a number of miles. As money was received each week, the line was extended.

This plan had two primary benefits in addition to the money raised. First, it unified the church family in supporting the youth trip. The whole project was one of cooperation because church contributions were combined with the funds that were raised in other ways. Second, the chart provided a great visual picture of the fund raiser. It was a focal point each Sunday as people came to church.

4. Pennies Make Sense—A contest was the sensible approach for a fund raiser in a church in Nevada. The group members pitted the men against the women in a race to collect and contribute the most pennies for the mission trip.

They set up a large, old-fashioned wooden scale with copper buckets in the church lobby. The men were to load one bucket with pennies; the women, the other. The young people also set up a display of the workcamp—brochures, maps and cultural symbols of the area. A sign above the display said, "Even pennies will pay our way to the workcamp."

The contest lasted eight weeks, and each Sunday the young people emptied the buckets, counted the pennies and prepared the next week's bulletin insert, which announced the results so far and kept up interest and enthusiasm.

Some people wanted to contribute but did not have pennies, so the kids accepted silver and bills and exchanged them at a bank.

The youth group spent an evening wrapping the pennies. The fun part was taking the wrapped coins to the bank—in exchange for $400.

5. Penny Saturday—Thinking "big" is ambitious, but sometimes thinking "small" is more beneficial. It was for a California youth group. The youth group members asked church families to part with their jars or boxes of pennies and spare change. They explained the goal of accumulating enough coins to be able to form a mile-long chain. The chain of pennies would help pay their way to a workcamp. It also symbolized the long road they had to travel to get to the site.

They announced well ahead of time that on a certain Saturday they would lay all the donated change on the church parking lot. Thanks to a good promotion crew, the coins came rolling in that Saturday.

The sun-baked coins lined up one by one made quite a spectacular sight and many people stayed to watch. By the end of the day the group had laid down $700 worth of coins, mostly pennies!

6. Free Carwash—Members of a youth group in Texas operated a "free" carwash that made big money. They didn't charge people to wash their cars. Instead, the members solicited sponsors who pledged a certain amount of money for each car washed. Then they washed as many cars as possible in the time they had.

It's important to publicize the carwash in the church and surrounding area so people will bring their cars. They parked the vehicles they were taking to the workcamp and decorated the vehicles with posters that said: "New Mexico or bust!" and "It's a long way to the New Mexico workcamp."

The youth group used multiple washing lines, with a work team on each line. The teams worked in two-hour shifts.

They also set up a donation box (just in case) and operated a simultaneous bake sale.

The drivers each were asked to sign their name and address on a sheet, so the kids had proof of the cars washed.

7. All-Night Bake Sale—Here's a bake sale with a little different twist. A youth group in Michigan made a good profit from an all-night baking party. They cooked items that were popular in their workcamp area such as biscuits and peach cobbler. They also cooked favorites such as chocolate chip and peanut butter cookies, brownies and hot fudge sauce.

The kids divided up the church directory, called every member of the church and asked for orders. From the orders they calculated how much of various ingredients they needed. Because of the size of their grocery order, a local grocer gave them a reduced price.

They met at the church early Friday evening and divided into various crews: mixers, bakers and packagers. They traded jobs throughout the night. They stopped to have breakfast together and then left to deliver all the goodies.

After the cloud of flour settled, some kids never wanted to see another chocolate chip or peanut butter cookie again, but they had a great time. It was a unifying experience to work together all night. Besides that, they made a lot of money for their mission trip.

8. Soup Sunday—A youth group in California sponsored a Soup Sunday as a fund raiser for its workcamp trip. The kids enlisted the help of a congregation member who was known for his good Italian cooking. After gathering all the ingredients he requested, they worked on Saturday to prepare the soup.

On "Soup Sunday" they made a special announcement in church. They asked three women who were considered the congregation's best cooks to come forward and sample the soup. These professional tasters were impressed and helped attract a big crowd after the service. They charged a minimal amount for a cup of soup and French bread, but made it clear that larger donations would be gladly accepted. The kids were servers. They dressed up in workcamp attire such as painter's caps, overalls, nail aprons and so on.

Everyone enjoyed the soup; and some people bought quarts of soup to take home.

9. Buy the Beard—This fund raiser takes little effort and earns 100 percent profit.

All you need to do is ask a youth sponsor to grow a beard, then sit back and let the comments roll in. Then simply begin two collections to allow people to voice their opinions about the youth sponsor growing a beard.

Advertise with posters and fliers that say: "Should the youth sponsor shave for the workcamp, or let his beard grow? You decide."

The kids in one group collected the money during the coffee hour. They wore signs on their backs so people would know to which side they were giving the money. These signs said "Shave It Off" or "Keep It On."

If you are lucky, someone will say he or she will "make up the difference, just to ensure that the youth sponsor will shave." Once word of that gets around, people start supporting the "Keep It On" side, knowing that their money will be doubled.

F. Workcamp Opportunities

The following organizations offer workcamp opportunities. Call or write to the organizations for costs or more information. (See Chapter 4 for questions to ask.) Many denominations also sponsor workcamps; call your denominational headquarters for more information.

Appalachia Service Project
Asbury Center
Boone and Watauga
Johnson City, TN 37601
(615) 928-1776

Coordinates and supervises home-repair projects such as dry walling and carpentry. Senior high youth groups must apply by November, and applications are approved on the basis of the organization's philosophy. Each project requires 40 to 60 participants. Each work team consists of four to seven people. This organization is associated with the United Methodist Church, but open to anyone.

Civil Defense and Disaster Response Agencies

Usually provide people who coordinate volunteer groups responding to natural disasters and emergency situations. The workcamp concept does not exist, but when needs arise, adults as well as young people are encouraged to volunteer their time, energy and materials. The agencies generally have access to tools and materials, but it helps when volunteers bring their own. Contact your local agencies for more information.

Confrontation Point Ministries
Box 50
Ozone, TN 37842
(615) 354-0292

Coordinates and supervises Missions Work Camps for low-income people living in the Cumberland Mountains of Tennessee. Only group applications (junior and senior high) are accepted. Each group works on its own project. Groups are trained for one day, work for four days and have a celebration and recreation day. Room, board and insurance are provided. The program includes devotions and worship. Overseas opportunities also are available.

DOOR (Denver Opportunity for Outreach and Reflection)
430 W. Ninth Ave.
Denver, CO 80204
(303) 892-1039

Arranges workcamp programs for Denver's low-income families through community agencies. Urban awareness is emphasized. Only group applications (junior high through college) are accepted, and one adult must accompany every five young people. Teams of up to 30 people work for one week on housing-rehabilitation projects. Room, board and materials are provided. DOOR is associated with Mennonite churches, but is open to anyone.

Evangelical Association for the Promotion of Education
Box 238
St. Davids, PA 19087
(215) 341-1722

Provides programs in the inner city of Philadelphia for church youth groups (junior high through college) to participate in housing re-habilitation, drama, outdoor worship, etc. Groups may propose their own agenda. Programs last two weeks; housing is provided for groups of up to 25 people, and groups must furnish meals. Workers should bring some tools and materials, depending on the project. EAPE is under the guidance of Anthony Campolo.

GROUP Workcamps
Box 481
Loveland, CO 80539
(303) 669-3836

Coordinates and supervises construction and home-repair projects throughout the United States. Only group applications are accepted, and one adult must accompany every five young people, ages 14-19. Each week-long workcamp involves 300 to 400 participants. Local agencies provide quality control. Activities are scheduled throughout the week, including evening interpretive programs. Room, board, insurance and materials are provided.

Habitat for Humanity
419 W. Church St.
Americus, GA 31709
(912) 924-6935

Provides supervision and planning for construction projects in a variety of locations, both inner city and rural, throughout the United States and Canada. Individuals must be 18 or older to apply. Smaller groups usually work on one project for one week. Housing is provided for participants. Long-term opportunities also are available in the United States and overseas.

Heifer Project International
Learning & Livestock Center
Route 2
Perryville, AR 72126
(501) 376-6836

Coordinates a 1,200-acre ranch that accommodates 1,500 animals which are raised and given to low-income farmers in the United States and overseas. Participants do chores at the ranch such as repairing fences, renovating barns, painting and so on. Work groups of up to 30 people should apply a year in advance, and provide one adult leader for every five young people. Participants must be in the ninth-grade or older. Workcamps last for one week, with usually only one group working during that week. The organization provides tools, materials, housing and a kitchen; participants must cook their meals. Groups are expected to hold a fund-raising project in their church or community for the organization before they start work at the ranch.

Intervarsity Missions
233 Langdon St.
Madison, WI 53703
(608) 257-0263

Provides college students (either individuals or groups) with many opportunities in overseas missions. These opportunities are meant to complement students' fields of study. Construction and medical assistance are among the variety of ministries of this nondenominational organization.

Missions By Involvement
Food for the Hungry
Box E
Scottsdale, AZ 85252
(800) 2-HUNGER

Arranges workcamp programs in Mexico and the Dominican Republic for people 15 or older. A 2,000-acre ranch in Mexico contains educational facilities and a store built by young people through this organization, and teams continue to build and minister to the people of Mexico there. Individuals or groups may apply, and one adult must accompany every five young people. Groups are trained for one weekend, then go to their work sites for one to three weeks.

Mountain TOP
Box 128
Altamont, TN 37301
(615) 692-3999

Coordinates and supervises home-repair projects such as roof and porch repair and outhouse construction in Appalachia. This program is open only to junior high, senior high and college groups. Work crews consist of six people, with one adult in each crew. Participants bring tools. Each project lasts for one week, and projects function from June until August.

Servant Events
Board for Youth Services
Lutheran Church-Missouri Synod
1333 S. Kirkwood Road
St. Louis, MO 63122
(314) 965-6000

Coordinates and supervises workcamps that involve home-repair projects. A primary purpose is a "Christlike style of servanthood." This program is open to youth groups or individuals age 14 or older. Work sites are located at various places throughout the United States. Room and board are provided.

SWAP (Sharing With Appalachian People)
Box 1507
Harlan, KY 40831
(606) 573-7846

Coordinates and supervises construction projects for low-income people. Only group applications (junior high through college) are accepted. Teams of 10 to 25 people work for one week; projects continue through the summer. Room and board are provided. Participants may be asked to bring some tools and materials. SWAP is associated with Mennonite churches, but is open to anyone.

Teen Missions
Box 1056
Merritt Island, FL 32952
(305) 453-0350

Trains and supervises teenagers to build churches, clinics, orphanages, etc. Individual participants age 13-22 must apply by December. Young people can choose from over 50 teams, including nine evangelism teams. Participants cover their travel costs; room and board are furnished. Projects last for two months, and many are overseas.

Voice of Calvary Ministries
1655 St. Charles St.
Jackson, MS 39209
(601) 353-1635

The Volunteer Group Program coordinates and supervises home-rehabilitation projects in the poor black communities of Mississippi. Teams of 10 to 30 young people (junior high and older) and adults work for one week, and there are activities in the evenings. Participants supply their own breakfast and dinner. Groups must submit a deposit and furnish one-third of the materials needed for each project; each homeowner furnishes one-third; and the organization furnishes the other one-third.

Volunteers in Mission
475 Riverside Drive, Room 1126
New York, NY 10115
(212) 870-2802

Matches established youth groups (junior and senior high) with workcamp programs within a particular synod. Over 100 project sites are available throughout the United States. The projects generally last from one to two weeks. The organization is associated with the Presbyterian Church (U.S.A.), but is open to anyone.

Youth With a Mission (YWAM)
Box 4600
Tyler, TX 75712
(214) 882-5591

Summer School of Training and Mercy Ministries both provide training, supervision and planning for various relief projects throughout the United States and overseas. Project locations are selected on the basis of a specific need, be it construction, medical assistance, agricultural training or food and clothing. Groups and individuals may apply. Participants age 15 or older are trained for about two weeks at one of 18 bases in the United States, and work for one week at the project location. Projects of up to or over a year also are available.

115545